THE IDEAS OF *Ayn Rand*

THE IDEAS OF Ayn Rand

RONALD E. MERRILL

Open  Court

Chicago and La Salle, Illinois

✼

OPEN COURT and the above logo are registered in the U.S. Patent and Trademark Office.

Copyright 1991 by Ronald E. Merrill

First printing 1991
Second printing 1993
Third printing 1995

Printed and bound in the United States of America.

Library of Congress Cataloging-in-Publication Data

Merrill, Ronald E., 1947-
        The Ideas of Ayn Rand / Ronald E. Merrill.
            p. cm.
        Includes bibliographical references and index.
        ISBN 0-8126-9157-1. — ISBN 0-8126-9158-X (pbk.)
        1. Rand, Ayn. I. Title
    B945.R233M47 1991   91-11283
    191—dc20   CIP

For Yoon

CONTENTS

Preface   xi

1 | THE CONTROVERSIAL AYN RAND   1

The Objectivist Movement   2
The 'Ayn Rand Cult': Fact and Fancy   3
The Great Schism   5
The Miracle of the Rose   6
The Resurrection of Ayn Rand   7
The Whole Rand   8

2 | RAND'S LIFE IN PRINT   11

Rand's Thinking in Context   15
The Evolution of Objectivism   17
The Randian Style   17

3 | THE NIETZSCHEAN PERIOD   21

The Nietzschean Vision   22
Literary Influences   27
Rand's Early Fiction   28
Red Pawn   30
Penthouse Legend   31
We the Living   33
The Theme   34
Trio for Heroes   35
A Cinematic Style   36
The Changes   37
The Failure of Nietzsche   40

4 | THE TRANSITION PERIOD   41

The Enigma of *Ideal*   41
Think Twice   44
The Fountainhead   45
The Break with Nietzsche   47
A Traditional Antithesis   50
The Impossible Villain   51
Intellectual Snobbery   52
A Seamless Patchwork   53
Acquital Unsatisfactory   54
The Embryo of Objectivism   55
Anthem   55
'The Simplest Thing in the World'   57

5 | FULL INTEGRATION   59

A Departure in Style   59
Judaic Symbolism   61
Plot, Plot, and Plot   62
The Technique of Philosophical Integration   63
Rand's Heroes: The Roots   66
Dagny Taggart and the Randian Woman   68
Francisco D'Anconia   71
Hank Rearden   72
Who *Is* John Galt?   73
Bit-Part Heroes   74
The Villains   74
The Secondary Heroes   76
The Branden Critique   79
Rand and Repression   80
The Randian Lovers   82
Paradox Resolved   84
Beyond the Taggart Terminal   85

6 | THE PHILOSOPHICAL PERIOD   87

Objectivism versus Academia   88
Metaphysical Roots   90

An Epistemological Radical   91
Rand's Theory of Concepts   93
The Analytic-Synthetic Dichotomy   96
Epistemology in Practice   97
The Objectivist Ethics   98
Ethics and Values: Two Lines of Argument   100
The Randian Argument   101
Ends and Ends in Themselves   102
The Means Test   104
Rand and the Aristotelian Legacy   105
From Is to Ought: Is There Aught, or
    Is All for Nought?   106
What is the Meaning of Life, Anyway?   110
The Objections to Objectivist Ethics   113
Simple Misrepresentations   113
From Leaking Lifeboats to the Asteroid Test   113
The Galt-Like Golfer   116
Robert Nozick versus the Count of Monte Cristo   117
Human Nature and Its Consequences   119
The Ethics of the Future   120
From Theory to How-To   122
Objectivist Esthetics   122
Esthetic Difficulties and Definitions   124

7 | THE POLITICAL PERIOD   127

A Political Odyssey   127
The Radical for Capitalism   130
The Goldwater Debacle   130
Roots of the New Conservatism   132
Rand's Critique of Conservatism   133
The Evolution of Libertarianism   135
The Essence of Libertarianism   135
Roots of the Political Conflict   136
Objectivism versus Libertarianism:
    The Case for the Plaintiff   138
Objectivism versus Libertarianism:
    The Case for the Defendant   140

Objectivism and the Theory of Government   141
Rand's View of Man and Society   144
The Final Decline   147
The Path Less Travelled   148

8 | THE FUTURE OF OBJECTIVISM   151

A Second Crusade?   151
Or the Ivory Tower?   153
The Schoolroom or the Polling Booth   155
Back to the Future   157
What Is to Be Done?   159
Life Support Systems   160
The Tactics of Sanction   161
The First of Their Return . . .   162

Notes   165

Bibliography   179

Index   187

PREFACE

Ideally a book should be left to justify itself. A preface, as Saint-Exupéry warned, is a dangerous expedient for an author, prone to slip into either apology or belligerence. Still, the reader is entitled to certain warnings and disclaimers. This book is not a biography of Ayn Rand; others have undertaken that task. Neither is it devoted to restatement or paraphrase of her ideas; Rand (unlike, say, Kant) explains her own views much more clearly than any commentator could. Readers seeking a first introduction to Objectivism will find it more profitable, and a great deal more entertaining, to read *Atlas Shrugged*.

The Ideas of Ayn Rand is aimed primarily, not at the professional philosopher, but at the lay reader who is familiar with Rand's work and interested in how it can be not only understood but extended. My objective is threefold. First, to give an account of the development of Ayn Rand's ideas—to explain where Objectivism came from. Second, to present a perspective of Objectivism as an organic whole, an integrated philosophy with an organized, hierarchical structure tied together by certain key themes. Third, to identify areas in which Ayn Rand's ideas are incomplete, and in some cases incorrect, and to suggest lines for the future expansion of Objectivism.

Scholars will probably find this work sadly deficient in the ceremonial apparatus of conventional academic debate. I must warn that this book was never intended to meet the standards of a formal scholarly monograph. Since I am a scientist, my approach is expository, rather than the dialectical or argumentive style traditional with philosophers. Again, as a scientist, I am primarily concerned with whether an idea is correct, rather than with who was the first to think of it. I have thus given short shrift to issues of precedence.

Objectivism, the subject of this work, has been for me not just a topic of study, but the organizing principle of my life for nearly 30 years. Thus I do not write about Objectivism as a disinterested party. But let me also set down for the record that at no time during her life did Ayn Rand designate me as her spokesman in any way whatsoever; nor, were she alive today, is it likely she would do so now. I oppose both those who believe Ayn Rand could never be wrong, and those who believe no one can be certain what is right.

I am grateful to many people who have instructed and assisted me in understanding Objectivism. But I wish specifically to thank David Kloepper, whose index to Objectivist literature was a valuable resource for my study, and Adam Reed, who brought to my attention the use of Jewish symbolism in Rand's work. I am also grateful to Robert W. Poole, Jr., for loaning me a copy of the first edition of *We the Living*. Tibor Machan, David Kelley, J. Roger Lee, and Douglas Rasmussen made valuable suggestions for improvement of the manuscript. The editorial assistance of David Ramsay Steele greatly strengthened the text. Of course none of these people should be held responsible for any errors in this book, which are wholly my own.

1 | THE CONTROVERSIAL AYN RAND

I was fifteen—a common age for converts to the ideas of Ayn Rand. Browsing in the library, I encountered a book called *Atlas Shrugged*. "A man who said he would stop the motor of the world—and did." What was it? Science fiction? Sounded intriguing, anyway, so I checked it out.

I opened it that evening and within a few pages I was hooked. The plot, the characters, above all the ideas—never had I encountered anything so exciting. It was not a book that I couldn't put down. On the contrary, I had to put it down every now and then because I would become so excited that I couldn't keep my eyes on the page. In the early morning hours I finally finished the book. I knew by then that my life had been changed permanently.

Thousands of other people, most of them young, have had much the same experience. The ideas of Ayn Rand exert a significant and increasing influence on our culture.

The success of her ideas certainly does not derive from the approbation of the intelligentsia. About the best that critics have been willing to say of *Atlas Shrugged* is that it is a ridiculous melodrama broken up by boring philosophical speeches. Yet the book has achieved astounding permanence. Walk into your local bookstore and you will find *Atlas Shrugged* on the shelves—certainly in paperback, and probably in hardbound also. Of the tens of thousands of books published in 1957, how many are still in print 30 years later?

But the direct popularity of Rand's books is only the visible part of the iceberg. Her ideas are appearing, though anonymously, in a growing portion of public discourse. On many fronts in modern intellectual life the subterranean influence of Objectivism can be detected. The resurgence of conservatism during the 1980s was to a significant extent powered by the quiet theft of Objectivist ideas. George Gilder's concept of the "altruistic entrepreneur" is a distorted form of Rand's insight that the entrepreneur is not and cannot be fully repaid in money for what he gives to society. Charles Murray's studies of the negative effects of welfare programs validate Rand's concept of the corrupting effect of the unearned. Meanwhile, on the other side of the political spectrum, liberals bemoan their loss of the intellectual initiative; they do not seem to realize, and if they do they certainly never admit, that it was Rand's attacks that demolished their positions.

THE OBJECTIVIST MOVEMENT

It is Objectivism which is achieving this influence, yet its creator receives little notice, let alone credit. It was not always so. In the 1960s there was an Objectivist movement, organized, growing, gaining converts continually. Centered around a monthly journal, *The Objectivist*, and a lecture organization, the Nathaniel Branden Institute, this movement began to recruit many of the 'best and brightest', particularly among college students. College professors, almost 100% left-liberal in those days, were horrified.

Those who did not experience it do not realize how violent the opposition to Objectivism was in the intellectual atmosphere of the Sixties. An anecdote from my own experience may be enlightening.

I enthusiastically recommended *Atlas Shrugged* to my college English teacher. She bought a copy, but did not finish reading it; she told me it was "boring". I heard no more about it until the next semester, when she told me the following story.

On a warm spring day her fiancé visited her apartment. Suddenly spotting *Atlas Shrugged* on her shelf, he said, "You don't want to read that", and without further ado he picked it up and pitched it out the open window. She ran to the window and saw that the book had fluttered to the grass near the building's gardener, who was mowing the lawn. He looked at it—saw the title—and went over it repeatedly with the power mower until it was chopped to confetti.

Such were the emotions aroused by the ideas of Ayn Rand. Many of my comrades in the movement could tell similar stories.

As the Sixties wore on the explosive growth of the organized Objectivist movement began to slow. Those of us who were students at the time could see that the movement was beginning to become less a spontaneous phenomenon, more an organized system. There was a trend toward a sort of intellectual centralization; it was made explicit that only Ayn Rand and a few of her close associates were to contribute original ideas to the movement. The rest of us were to act merely as 'transmission belts' to carry these ideas to the uninitiated. We were even forbidden to call ourselves 'Objectivists'; instead we were instructed that we were humble 'students of Objectivism'. At the same time, some disquieting signs began to appear. An increasing number of 'true believers' appeared among our ranks. Objectivist doctrine seemed in danger of hardening into dogma. Dissenters, including some of the movement's leaders, began to be formally 'excommunicated'.

THE 'AYN RAND CULT': FACT AND FANCY

Several writers have described the Objectivist movement as a snake-pit of cultism, emotional repression, and thought control.[1] The lurid picture painted by these authors may mislead younger readers.

I was an active participant in the movement in the Sixties, including stints as leader of Objectivist groups at MIT and the University of Oregon. On numerous occasions I visited New York for NBI functions. Never did I encounter a single one of the cape-wearing, cigarette-holder-wielding cultists who were allegedly so omnipresent in the movement. Certainly I did meet a number of self-appointed guardians of ideological purity. But I, and the vast majority of my friends in the movement, regarded these characters with amused tolerance rather than quaking fear.

It should be kept in mind that most published descriptions of the Objectivist movement were written by people who detested it.

The leading purveyor of the "Ayn Rand Cult" allegations is Murray Rothbard, whose polemic[2] describes an Objectivist movement that I somehow never saw. Some of his assertions are exaggerations (for example, "Rand's whole-hearted endorsement of Goldwater, Nixon, and Ford"). Others are merely astonishing. That the NBI recommended reading list functioned as "an Index of Permitted Books" was a secret well kept from me and the Objectivists I knew; most of us were enthusiastic admirers of Rothbard's own *Man, Economy, and State.* The smokers I knew within the movement would certainly have been surprised and pleased if they'd only known that "smoking, according to the cult, was a moral obligation"; they were used to being criticized by the rest of us for irrational and self-destructive behavior.

Rothbard recites a series of anecdotes about unnamed people—"young Randians", "a Randian girl", "high-ranking Randians"—to back up his claims of cultist-like behavior. I met some fairly flaky specimens in the movement, but none as bizarre as his acquaintances. Maybe I just didn't travel in the right circles.

The central point of Rothbard's essay is the claim that the Randian movement was strictly "hierarchical" and "totalitarian". Certainly there were—and are—those within it who would like to make it so. But let me cite an anecdote of my own. In the mid-Sixties, a friend of mine took some questions to Nathaniel Branden personally. This direct approach was criticized by another student of Objectivism, who said he should have gone through channels. ("First take it to Harry Binswanger. If he thinks it's worthwhile, he'll allow you to see Allan Gotthelf, and if he . . .") Branden, on being informed of this, called that attitude "intellectual feudalism"—which of course it was. *That* is how the "Randian cultists" were regarded within the movement.

But Nathaniel Branden seems to have forgotten incidents like this; indeed, his memoirs[3] have given a great boost to the legend of the Ayn Rand Cult. The Objectivist movement that I saw from my worm's-eye view was very different—and, apparently, much healthier—than the inner circle around Rand. That hotbeds of cultism existed I do not deny, though I never happened to encounter them. That the movement itself was a cult simply is not true. I cannot but suspect that when Branden finds it difficult to remember a student of Objectivism who was not a "fanatical repressor",[4] his recollection is colored by his bitter memories of the Great Schism.

THE GREAT SCHISM

Unknown to most of us, there was a worm eating at the heart of the movement. For years Rand had been carrying on a sordid sexual affair with her leading disciple, Nathaniel Branden. The reluctant consent of their respective spouses had been extorted by Rand's extraordinary skill in personal argument—and by their admiration of and gratitude to Rand. In 1968 this unstable relationship exploded when Rand discovered that Branden had secretly taken up with a younger woman. Outraged and humiliated, Rand denounced Branden for alleged philosophical and financial improprieties and expelled him from the movement. In response, the Brandens revealed part of the truth, though the full story was concealed until the publication of Barbara Branden's biography of Rand in 1986.

The result in 1968 was the disintegration of the movement. The Nathaniel Branden Institute was disbanded. Branden himself moved across the country and went into full-time practice as a psychotherapist. Gradually his psychological theories trended toward the California Standard 'get in touch with your feelings' approach, and he became much less involved with, and occasionally critical of, Objectivism.[5] Most of the movement's true believers left and moved on to real cults. Some of the rank and file clustered around the rump movement in New York. Others joined the nascent 'libertarian' political movement which was beginning to stir, especially in California. Many of us simply abandoned all confidence in our leaders and concentrated silently on living as Objectivists.

The movement was effectively destroyed. Yet, like an ideological neutron bomb, the Great Schism destroyed the idols but left the ideas intact. While Objectivism faded from the public eye, young people continued to read *Atlas Shrugged* and find that these ideas made sense. They accepted Objectivism if not in whole then in part, and as the years went by they graduated from college and began to take their places as potential intellectual leaders. Rand's ideas were carried with them.

Rand herself, however, remained swept under the rug. The current renaissance in conservative thought owes much to the vitality of ideas imported from Rand's work, yet she remains anathema to the traditional Right. The burgeoning libertarian movement has deep roots in Objectivism and owes much, if not most, of its strength to the impetus provided by Ayn Rand; rather than credit her, most libertarian intellectuals seem inclined to hide her in the basement.

THE MIRACLE OF THE ROSE

It was no doubt inevitable, considering the dramatic events of Ayn Rand's life, that attention would focus as much on her character as on her thinking. The titillating details of her personal—especially sexual—behavior have caught the interest of the public.

I cannot testify much as to Ayn Rand's personality. I met her several times, briefly, at public appearances; that is all. But I, like almost everyone else who met her, found it an unforgettable experience to talk to her. "She *radiates* intelligence," I told a friend. It was a good metaphor. On a stage, seen from the audience, this short, dumpy, ugly old woman with a dense Russian accent was intellectually exciting, but personally unimpressive. But when you approached her closely, an inverse-square law took hold, and her mind shone out at you through her incredible eyes with an intensity that seemed almost physically sizzling. I can easily understand that bright young people would give anything to orbit around this stellar intellect, even though it burned away their own personalities.

The confessions of Barbara and Nathaniel Branden paint an ugly picture of Ayn Rand's treatment of her disciples. If we accept these accounts, Rand was routinely inconsiderate and often cruel. She stifled intellectual independence and crushed originality. Ultimately she became a hypocrite who violated in her own life the ideals she had devised and explained to her followers.

The Brandens, though they admit to being accomplices as well as victims of Rand, still seem not to recognize fully the influence they and the other members of 'the Collective' had on her. To the extent that they passively accepted the sort of intellectual bullying of which they accuse her, they corrupted her—as slaves always corrupt their masters. Surrounded as she was by the distorting mirrors of her sycophantic admirers, it is not surprising that Rand lost touch with reality.

Of course in the end nothing can excuse Ayn Rand's betrayals of her own principles. But let us reject the almost instinctive human tendency to judge ideas by the personality of the thinker, to evaluate a creation according to the character of the creator. We must acknowledge the 'miracle of the rose'—beauty growing out of dung. Richard Wagner was a philanderer and swindler who, between music-dramas, wrote scurrilous anti-semitic pamphlets. Renowned scientists, from Johannes Stark to the Joliot-Curies, have willingly served totalitarian regimes. Thomas Jefferson owned slaves.

The human mind finds a deep frustration in these contradictions between a creator's personal character and his work. One sees this clearly in Nathaniel Branden's memoirs. As a boy, he thought Ayn Rand must be perfect, to match her books. He dismissed any evidence to the contrary. When, finally, painful experience forced him to confront her faults, he decided her philosophy was imperfect because she was imperfect. Ayn Rand promoted emotional repression in real life, he asserts; therefore the same attitude must be present in her books. Again, he dismisses evidence to the contrary.

When I began this book, *The Ideas of Ayn Rand* was merely a working title. But I now think it perfectly expresses my desire to move the focus of discussion from judgment on Rand as a person to understanding and evaluation of the ideas she created.

THE RESURRECTION OF AYN RAND

In recent years interest in Ayn Rand has begun to revive. Some of the basic prerequisites for the study of Rand and her ideas have been laid into place. Barbara Branden's biography, *The Passion of Ayn Rand*, made available for the first time the key information necessary to understand the intellectual development of this extraordinary woman. A bibliography and research guide by Mimi Gladstein (*The Ayn Rand Companion*) provides a useful resource. Harry Binswanger's *Ayn Rand Lexicon* offers convenient access to many of Rand's key arguments. An introductory critique of her thought has been published (*The Philosophic Thought of Ayn Rand*, edited by Douglas Den Uyl and Douglas Rasmussen).

Most important, a full volume of Rand's work—plays, stories, and outtakes—has been published posthumously by Leonard Peikoff (*The Early Ayn Rand*). As we shall see, much of this previously unavailable work served Rand as sketches or test beds for her major projects, so that it offers valuable insights into the evolution of her ideas.

Much, however, remains to be done. Scholars have not even begun to scratch the surface in the study of Rand's place in twentieth-century thought. Who influenced her thinking? Whose thinking did she in turn influence? How did she fit into her time, and how did she change it? As for the professional philosophers, they have examined her contribution to philosophy in only the most superficial manner. They have not yet begun to grapple with the full implications of her ideas, especially in the field of ethics.

The Whole Rand

What is needed most at this time is an overview and analysis of Rand's thinking, examining her ideas and their implications, and suggesting lines for further exploration. This is what I have attempted to provide. Too much criticism and analysis of Rand's thinking has been piecemeal.

I have chosen to use a developmental analysis of Rand's work. Commonly her critics, as well as her supporters, have based their discussion on her philosophical and political essays, with an occasional reference to Galt's speech in *Atlas Shrugged*. This is inadequate. Rand's thought is by no means simple or superficial, and her pellucid prose can propel the reader to her conclusions so quickly that he may miss the deep layers of subtle reasoning that form the foundation of her philosophy. It is therefore essential to analyze Rand's fiction works in depth, and to study the development of her ideas chronologically. Often one can fully understand what she has accepted only by contrasting it with what she has rejected.

Rand's philosophical roots in the Aristotelian tradition are well known. Not so well understood is her ambivalent attitude toward Friedrich Nietzsche. Rand started her career as a follower of this enigmatic philosopher. By looking at Rand's work chronologically, we can trace a fascinating intellectual odyssey. Her ethical, political, and esthetic values, woven together in a complex manner, were developed by a process of rejection and revision of the Nietzschean vision. The Objectivist's knee-jerk fear of being tarred with the Nietzschean brush has inhibited an objective evaluation of this process.

No less interesting is the way in which Ayn Rand's personal dilemma, her life-long struggle against a hostile intellectual climate, affected her philosophy and her art. As we shall see, a corollary of this determined resistance was her consistent theme, prominent in all her fiction, of integrity and loyalty to values.

Ayn Rand was not just a philosopher, but a philosophical system-builder; not merely an intellectual, but an artist. Only her relentless consistency made it possible for her to integrate these varied aspects of her work. It is this total integration which makes her ideas so compelling, which hits the first-time reader with that feeling, 'But of course! How could I have ever thought otherwise?' Unfortunately, it is too easy to take this certainty for granted, and thus fail to examine and understand the architectural ingenuity which underlies it.

One ought not to miss either the sheer fun that was always a part of Ayn Rand's writing. Her pleasure in the paradoxical, the bizarre, the shocking, enhanced the talent that made her such a superb teacher. Satirizing Gertrude Stein, slipping the needle to collectivist science with a casual allusion to the "seventeen illustrious inventors of the candle", or slyly hiding a talmudic theme in *Atlas Shrugged*, she entertains as she instructs.

Several decades have now passed since that December night on which I read *Atlas Shrugged* for the first time. In that interval I have reread the book many times; I lost count years ago. As I have grown older, many of the books that I loved and admired as a youth have lost their charm for me. They seem oversimplified, naive, unsophisticated. But not *Atlas Shrugged*. On the contrary, each time I read it, even now, I find new concepts, new depths of subtlety, new insights. No writer has ever exceeded Rand in clarity of exposition. But this does not mean that her thinking is simple. Brief though it is, I hope that the treatment which follows will give some indication of the profound and subtle ingenuity of Ayn Rand's thought.

2 | RAND'S LIFE IN PRINT

A serious biographical study of Ayn Rand is beyond the scope of this book.[1] However, a brief summary of her life will help to place in context the chronological development of her ideas. In addition, some appreciation of the personal ordeals she endured is necessary if one is to fully comprehend the source of key elements in her thinking.

Rand, born in 1905 as Alyssa (or Alice) Rosenbaum, was the daughter of a bourgeois Jewish family in St. Petersburg. Like many highly intelligent children, she found school boring, had difficulty making friends, and was more interested in the ideas and people she discovered by her reading than in her own family. At the age of nine she resolved to become a writer. Overall, her childhood was comfortable and her parents did not obstruct her intellectual development.

Unfortunately, this was the only peace she was ever to know. Alice was nine years old, enjoying her first ecstatic taste of the West on a vacation in Switzerland, when the lights of Europe began to go out. The Rosenbaums fled back to Russia to endure the uncertainties and privations of World War I. This was followed by the Russian Revolution, the Bolshevik *coup*, the Red Terror, and a lengthy civil war. Then came the inexorable crushing of all free thought as Russia was enslaved by the Communists. The Rosenbaums' family business was expropriated, and the family, after gradually eating its savings, lived in grinding poverty.

During this hellish period, in which the teenage girl lived with the fear of starvation, of disease, and of Siberia, she worked on the development of her literary abilities. She outlined plays and novels (though she did not actually write them). She read widely, admiring Rostand and Schiller and above all Victor Hugo, while disliking Russian authors, George Sand, and Shakespeare. She also became acquainted with the philosophy of Aristotle—and the ideas of Friedrich Nietzsche.

Shortly after graduating from college, where she majored in history, Rand succeeded in leaving the USSR and came to the United States. This fortunate escape was not without its disadvantages. Rand was cut off from her Russian heritage and had to master a new language—a serious handicap for the aspiring writer. She was also a stranger in a strange land, deprived of whatever comfort she had once had from friends and family. In addition her position as a new immigrant was precarious both legally and economically. It was not for several years that she was securely placed as an American citizen.

Rand supported herself in a variety of jobs, eventually succeeding in breaking into the fledgling movie industry as a writer of scenarios. As we shall see, this apprenticeship served her well and had a strong influence on her style.

The 1930s were no easier for Rand. Perhaps the only bright spot was her happy marriage to Frank O'Connor, an unsuccessful actor. During the decade she produced, in addition to some unpublished material, the novels *We the Living* and the novelette *Anthem*. Neither was a success at the time. The play *Night of January 16th* had a modest commercial success, though unavoidable compromises with the producer made it artistically frustrating. But Rand could not earn a living from her writing, and had to continue working at other jobs. This was the Great Depression, and she and her husband had often to wonder where the rent money was coming from.

The thirties were also the 'Red Decade'. The Left was riding high; the traditional Right was helpless, impotent, and reduced to frustrated reaction. The intellectual and social environment was savagely hostile to Rand's ideas, and the situation became increasingly worse throughout most of her lifetime.

Her second novel, *The Fountainhead*, published in 1943, was rejected by a dozen publishers. But when it finally saw print it became a best-seller and gave Rand for the first time some degree of financial security. It also gave her significant intellectual stature, placing her among the tiny group of thinkers who were laying the foundation for a renewal of the Right—people such as Isabel Paterson, Ludwig von Mises, and Friedrich von Hayek. Rand's ideas began to attract attention, and she began to attract disciples, including Nathaniel and Barbara Branden in the early 1950s. Meanwhile she was working on her magnum opus, *Atlas Shrugged*.

But the 1950s were also the heyday of liberalism. Though outright communism or socialism was out of style except in the intelligentsia, American culture was firmly in the grip of the 'moderate' Left. Liberalism totally dominated the world of ideas—a conservative professor, a conservative journal, a novel presenting a conservative viewpoint—all these were rarities. (In the academic world, a libertarian intellectual was not just a rarity but a freak of nature, like a two-headed calf.[2]) Under the Eisenhower administration a certain amount of public lip service was paid to conservative political values, but for a serious writer to be anything but left-wing was almost a contradiction in terms. Rand had not even the comfort of belonging to the tiny band of brothers, clustered around William F. Buckley, who formed the embryo of modern conservatism. She could not be fitted into the mold of traditional, religion-based conservatism.

It was the publication of *Atlas Shrugged* in 1957 that marked the real beginning of what might be called the 'Ayn Rand Phenomenon'. The book was an unlikely best-seller: An immense tome, laden with lengthy lectures on philosophy and politics, half science fiction and half melodrama, and challenging violently all the most cherished beliefs of the typical reader. Yet it was a best-seller, and indeed even today, more than 30 years later, one can walk into Dalton's and find the hardbound edition as well as the paperback on the shelf.

Atlas Shrugged had an immense appeal to young people, influencing many, such as George Gilder, who later returned to more traditional creeds. Gradually a hard core of 'Objectivist' college students formed. They read and re-read Rand's books, argued ferociously with their enemies and with one another, proselytized for 'converts', and spontaneously formed clubs and discussion groups.

There was clearly a market for Objectivism, a hunger for more of these ideas, and Nathaniel and Barbara Branden began in 1960 to satisfy the need with the creation of the Nathaniel Branden Institute (NBI). Rand and Branden began publishing *The Objectivist Newsletter* (which evolved into *The Objectivist* and later devolved into the *Ayn Rand Letter*). The taped lectures provided by NBI unified the various local groups of Objectivists and began the building of a national network of contacts. The Sixties were the Golden Age of Objectivism, as what had been a scattering of isolated thinkers coalesced into an important intellectual movement. The liberal establishment within the universities were forced, to their fury, to deal with challenges to their ideas from an increasing number of Objectivist students. The resurgent conservatives found, to their evident annoyance, that the brightest and most enthusiastic young people on the Right were adherents of, or at least much influenced by, this abhorrent, atheistic philosophy. The real danger to the Objectivist movement, however, came from within. So long as she was a single voice crying in the wilderness Ayn Rand, that quintessential individualist, was spared from any conflict between ideological purity and human relationships. As leader of an intellectual movement, she began to encounter the only kind of opposition she could not face. Any disagreement from her colleagues, friends, or students was a threat to the purity of her system, a portent of schism. Students at NBI lectures began to whisper rumors of 'excommunications'. Major figures in the movement, such as John Hospers and Edith Efron, were cast out.[3]

Finally the catastrophe came. In 1969 Rand's most important protégé and closest friend, Nathaniel Branden, was 'excommunicated', along with his wife Barbara, in an extraordinarily bitter conflict. Although the full story of the messy sexual affair that caused the break did not come out at the time, enough was exposed to irretrievably damage the personal reputations of both Rand and her former protégés.[4] NBI perforce collapsed, and the Objectivist network fissioned into pro-Rand and pro-Branden factions, with a considerable loss of mass as many students, disillusioned with the behavior of their teachers, left the movement altogether.

The majority of Rand's closest disciples—the inner circle known as 'the Collective'—took her side in the controversy, a tribute to her personal and intellectual charisma since most of them were relatives of the Brandens. An attempt was made to continue the work of NBI under a new name, but without the driving force of Nathaniel Branden and the business acumen of Wilfred Schwartz, NBI's manager, it was impossible to continue. Even *The Objectivist* could not be maintained. Rand, a slow and scrupulously careful writer, was unable to produce articles fast enough to support regular publication. Her remaining assistants could not contribute enough material of a quality to meet her exacting standards.

In the 1970s Rand's output declined to a dribble of unimportant articles in the *Ayn Rand Letter*. She became increasing isolated, gradually breaking ties with several of her remaining adherents. The death of her husband was a painful blow. Now an old woman and in ill health, she had little new left to say, and in 1975 she ceased writing almost entirely, continuing only her annual talks at Boston's Ford Hall Forum until her death in 1982.

RAND'S THINKING IN CONTEXT

Rand's life was, if not tragic, certainly difficult. From childhood she faced almost continuous stress and struggle. Economically, the first half of her life was precarious at best. Socially, she was cut off from her family by exile, from friends by her beliefs and attitudes, from children by her own choice; only her marriage was successful, and that only for a time. Her husband, Frank O'Connor, was a pleasant and likeable man but far from being her intellectual equal. Though she loved him deeply, her affair with Branden hurt Frank badly and his later years were marred by alcoholism.

Rand was a genius, but a genius doomed by her sex, and by her birth in the wrong time, to be in violent conflict with her environment. To understand this is to realize that—in a personal context—the central theme of Rand's life is her struggle with despair. She fought for decades, alone against the world, a battle as horrible as any endured by her fictional heroes. The constant thread which runs through all of her work is the problem of the moral individual trapped in an evil society. This was Rand's own dilemma in life.

Crucial to any deep understanding of Rand's intellectual development is the realization that Rand was almost completely alienated from the society in which she lived. She saw herself, with no small justification, as being a lone figure of reason and morality in a viciously evil culture. All of her major works of fiction deal with the same theme: the able and moral person trapped in an evil and oppressive society. How is he to survive? How can he preserve his psychological health? How can he triumph?

To one with this perspective on life, there is constant danger that resolution will degrade into repression, that alienation will evolve into paranoia. Rand recognized this hazard and explored it in her novels. Even so, in the end she succumbed to it herself.

'Repression', in something approaching the Freudian sense of the word—a denial or cutting-off of emotions from one's consciousness—was an important part of Objectivist theory. It was regarded as not just a psychological phenomenon, but at least potentially a moral offense, for repression of emotions can lead to denial of facts. And, for an Objectivist, refusal to face reality is a cardinal sin.

Nonetheless, repression was also prominent in practice among some Objectivists, notably including Ayn Rand herself. An unwillingness to face unpleasant emotions—and consequently, an unwillingness to face unpleasant facts—was already evident in Rand's behavior in the Sixties. Toward the end of her life, when her extraordinary intellect had been reduced to a dull glow in the ashes of her deteriorating body, Rand seems to have repressed so much pain that she began to lose touch with reality.[5]

As we shall see in discussing her novels, particularly *The Fountainhead* and *Atlas Shrugged*, Rand was well aware of the phenomenon of repression, and of its dangers, and had much counsel to offer on dealing with it. Critics who extrapolate her character from unpleasant anecdotes of her behavior in her declining years are suppressing (if not repressing) the full context of her life. And whatever the final judgment of Ayn Rand as a person, to characterize her as a high priestess of emotional repression wrongs her as a novelist and philosopher.

THE EVOLUTION OF OBJECTIVISM

Ayn Rand attempted to present herself as having started her adult life as an Objectivist. She claimed that she always held these beliefs, though she gradually expanded and improved her understanding. This was a falsehood.

Rand, at the time she wrote *We the Living*, was definitely an ethical Nietzschean. As her thinking developed, she began to abandon the emotionalism of Nietzsche for the rationalism of Objectivism. At the same time, her sense of life—at least as expressed in her writing—changed from one of existential despair to one of hope and confidence.

This can be seen by the progression of her four novels. In *We the Living* the struggle is between good (represented by Kira, Leo, and Andrei) and evil (the Communist State)—and evil wins. *Anthem* deals with the same fight, but this time the good is triumphant. *The Fountainhead* progresses further; now the conflict is between the good (Roark) and the imperfect (Dominique and Wynand). With *Atlas Shrugged* Rand dismisses the importance of evil entirely, and the conflict is between good and good (the strikers versus the scabs).

After the completion of her fictional output Rand went through a brief sterile period of severe depression before turning to non-fiction. She elaborated and systematized the philosophy of Objectivism, but added few major innovations to the ideas she had presented in *Atlas Shrugged*.

THE RANDIAN STYLE

Ayn Rand was one of the most innovative writers of the twentieth century, and it is worth noting some of the outstanding aspects of her unique style. Rand's writing is characterized by the following qualities:

Paradox. Rand's conscious and explicit commitment to logical consistency is a most obvious trait. One way in which it shows up in her fiction is her predilection for paradox. Repeatedly she challenges the reader with contradictions to be resolved. Sometimes the paradox appears in a major theme of the work; in *Think Twice*, for instance, a rich altruist, the benefactor of many people, turns out to be a vile sadist, and the recipients of his help the victims of torture. Sometimes paradox is a plot device: the scientific genius who works as an unskilled railroad laborer. Sometimes it appears in characterization; recall the scene in which Dagny Taggart admires Rearden's appearance of "ruthless asceticism"—at a moment when he has just been fantasizing a sexual assault on her. Or it may appear in the background—as in *Red Pawn*, where the Soviet prison is located in an old Russian Orthodox monastery with religious murals on the walls.

Épater les Bourgeois. Rand takes an almost childish delight in defying the conventions and shocking the reader. This is true not only in her presentation of philosophical principles ("The Virtue of Selfishness") but in her social attitudes (making a heroine out of a sexually unconventional forger in *Penthouse Legend*, for instance) and in her literary style (deliberately mixing melodrama, science fiction, and heavy philosophical discourses in *Atlas Shrugged*). Perhaps the classic example (though it might better be described as *épater l'intelligentsia*) is her essay on fiction technique in which she selects passages to show how Mickey Spillane is superior in style to Thomas Wolfe.

Surprise. Again, Rand took great delight in surprising and astonishing her readers. In her short story, 'The Simplest Thing in the World', Rand describes what seems to have been her own plotting technique: Think of an obvious, trite bromide of a theme—and give it a totally unexpected twist. Nathaniel Branden has described (in *Who Is Ayn Rand?* and *Judgment Day*) Rand's personal pleasure in the dénouement of *Atlas Shrugged*, in which the villains torture the hero—to force him to become dictator of the country. This habit of reversing clichés gives Rand's work much of its freshness and impact.

Visual imagery. Rand's experience writing for the movies shows up strongly in her literary style. Take for example Andrei's suicide in *We the Living*. The scene is strikingly visual—the silent room, the burning of Kira's clothing, the loading of the pistol. Then there is the movie-like dissolve from the silence to the band playing in Andrei's funeral procession, with the ironic counterpoint of the marching women's mundane and cynical conversation. The whole sequence could be translated to the screen with scarcely any revision. All of Rand's fiction shows this cinematic obsession with visual imagery.

Psychological insight. Rand has the faculty, rare among even the best writers, of getting into the minds of all her characters. She seldom falls into the trap (Ellsworth Toohey is the only major exception) of making a character do something 'just because' he is bad or good or whatever. Few novelists have surpassed, or even equalled, Rand's ability to make a character not only believable but understandable.

Moral focus. Though Rand is a figure of the twentieth century, her books have very much the flavor of the nineteenth. This stems from her choice of plot-themes. Any serious fiction is centered on a conflict within the central protagonist. What can be the source of this conflict? Roughly speaking—there are of course many exceptions!—one might make the following generalization. In the eighteenth century, novels tended to focus on 'manners' as a source of conflict: the hero wants to do something, but the dictates of custom forbid it. In the nineteenth century, the conflict tends to be moral in nature: the hero wants to do something, but his moral principles forbid it. In the twentieth century, the conflict tends to be psychological: the hero wants to do something, but is incapable because of his neurotic problems. In this analysis, Rand is quite definitely a nineteenth-century writer rather than a twentieth-century writer, in that the focus of her books is on moral issues rather than psychological problems.

Philosophical Themes. It takes some courage to write a novel about philosophy. Again, Rand in doing this is more of the last century than this one. The illustration of ethical principles by fictional action is today casually dismissed as 'didactic writing' or 'morality play'. (Unless, that is, the ethics advocated are left-wing in sympathy.) Rand's essays on philosophy within the novels, presented as speeches by her characters, are universally denounced by literary critics. Oddly enough these are the same professors who have no problem with the use of the same technique by writers like Tolstoy and Mann—and who sneer at students who find the sermons in Dante heavy going.

With this overview as background, we are ready to proceed to a detailed analysis of Rand's works, developed along chronological lines.

3 | THE NIETZSCHEAN PERIOD

The 'official' line on Friedrich Nietzsche's influence on Ayn Rand is that she briefly flirted with his ideas in college. She was attracted by Nietzsche's view of the heroic in man and his denunciation of collectivism and altruism. But she soon discovered Nietzsche's explicit repudiation of reason, and "that finished him as an intellectual ally."[1]

By Rand's own account she quickly and completely abandoned Nietzsche's philosophy, and developed her own philosophical ideas under the sole influence of Aristotle. This turns out not to be the case. During the first part of her career Rand's writings are clearly and explicitly Nietzschean—so much so that even her later substantial textual revisions were insufficient to conceal the evidence. It was not until the late 1930s that Rand finally broke with Nietzsche, and this break is an important theme in *The Fountainhead*.

During this Nietzschean period of her career Rand, as a new immigrant to the United States, developed her writing skills and began the effort to express her ideas in fiction vehicles. But the very expression challenged, and ultimately refuted, much of what she believed. With the completion of *We the Living* it became clear that she could not integrate her philosophy with her art; there was something wrong in Nietzsche, something that imposed on her stories either a tragic sense of life, or an optimism that threatened to degenerate into mere frivolity. It was in this crucible that Objectivism was smelted.

THE NIETZSCHEAN VISION

Many critics of Objectivism have casually assumed that it is merely a variant of Nietzsche's philosophy. Objectivism's defenders have indignantly denied the charge. Few on either side have displayed much familiarity with the actual ideas of that notoriously obscure and difficult thinker, Friedrich Nietzsche. Mostly he is described in vague terms as an advocate of 'selfishness' and inventor of the 'superman' who built the ideological foundation for Naziism.

Since Nietzsche unquestionably influenced Rand's development, it will pay us to examine his philosophy briefly. What did he actually advocate? What attracted Rand to his ideas, and what, in the end, drove her to repudiate them?

To begin with, Nietzsche viewed himself as leading the opposition to one of history's most influential philosophers, Immanuel Kant. Nietzsche accused Kant of attempting to set limits to the validity of reason as a means of rescuing Christian, altruistic morality. He agreed with Kant that reason and altruism were incompatible. Unlike Kant, he was prepared to jettison religion and altruism, so Nietzsche rejected Kant's attack on reason. Rand adopted this view of Kant as her own, and never abandoned it. Like Nietzsche, to the end of her life she considered Kant her intellectual arch-enemy. (She is said to have admitted, however, that she never actually read any of Kant's works herself.)

Though Nietzsche regarded himself as, in a sense at least, a defender of reason, he extended the common conception of reason to include the entire capability of the human entity: Not just deductive reasoning, but intuition, imagination, perception, and feeling were to him included in 'reason'. In developing Objectivism Rand rejected Nietzsche's idea that emotion is actually a form of reason. However, she retained the basic idea behind Nietzsche's concept of reason, the idea that human beings are unitary, that mind, soul, and body are inherently inseparable. This viewpoint is at the root of Rand's rejection of the 'mind-body dichotomy'. For her, as for Nietzsche, there is no inherent separation between mind and body. Note how Randian this quotation from Nietzsche sounds:

I have my word to say to those who despise the body. I am not asking them to learn better or teach better, but merely to say farewell to their body—and so be silent.[2]

Since there is no separation between mind and body, there is none between reason and emotion. Emotions may not be tools of cognition, but in the well-integrated person they do not conflict with reason. Here, for instance, is a passage from Rand's journal, written in 1934:

It may be considered strange and denying my own supremacy of reason—that I start with a set of ideas—then want to study in order to support them, and not vice-versa, that is, not study and derive my ideas from that. But these ideas, to a great extent, are the result of a subconscious instinct, which is a form of unrealized reason. All instincts are reason, essentially, or *reason is instincts made conscious.* The "unreasonable" instincts are diseased ones. This—for the study of psychology. For the base of the reconciliation of reason and emotions.[3]

One corollary to Nietzsche's expanded notion of human reason is the danger of being ruled by one's 'passions'. If emotions are to contribute to reasoning they must be held under strict control. Though Rand developed her own theory of emotion, her fiction, as we shall see, emphasized to the end heroic emotional control, sometimes characterized, incorrectly, as repression.

The logical next step for Nietzsche was the utter repudiation of religion and the supernatural, and man's acceptance of human life as an end in itself. The Nietzschean 'superman' accepts the obligation to make the most of himself, to constantly develop and improve his ability, courage, and creative will. Nobody can fully understand Rand's thinking without realizing that this emphasis on personal ability and strength of character, on what one is and is becoming, lies at the root of her morality, as it did for Nietzsche.

Finally, Nietzsche is compelled by his view of reason to proceed 'beyond good and evil'. It is not sufficient to repudiate the authority of priests. No exterior moral authority may be recognized, since 'reason' is not objective for Nietzsche, it is personal. Thus the 'superman' must be a law unto himself—philosophically, and therefore socially. But what if two people's 'reasoned' views are in conflict? Then the only resolution lies in force. Hence the 'will to power'; the 'superman' establishes the correctness of his views by forcing them upon those who disagree. This leads, obviously, to a social hierarchy, with the superman at the top and the 'masses' at the bottom. The morality of Judeo-Christian altruism is a 'slave morality'; the superman and those who aspire to that title must follow a morality of 'masters', a morality focussed on power. This sentiment seems to have caused Rand some queasiness from the start, and she later explicitly repudiated it.

Nietzsche's political views were confused at best. He, like Rand, knew what he was against—socialism and statism—far better than he knew what he was for. He was a perceptive opponent of the Marxist vision, though, as events turned out, too optimistic:

> [Socialism] desires a degree of political power as high as despotism has ever had. Indeed, it out rivals all the past in that it aims at the complete annihilation of the individual . . . it can hope to exist only here and there and only for a short time by means of extreme terrorism.[4]

Let it not be thought, however, that Nietzsche was an advocate of egoism. His concern was with the welfare of the race more than of the individual. This was at the root of his concept of the 'superman'.

Nietzsche, like most intellectuals of his time, was profoundly influenced by the concept of evolution. He believed passionately in the evolution of the human species into a higher order of being—the 'superman' (or 'overman', as the term *Übermensch* is sometimes translated)—a being who would be to man what humans are to apes. Unlike the Social Darwinists, however, Nietzsche saw this evolution as occurring not through 'survival of the fittest' and natural selection, but through 'sublimation'—the effort of the individual human being to make himself into something higher. He was, in fact—not a Social Darwinist, but, shall we say, a Social Lamarckist. Just as Lamarck's giraffe lengthened its neck by striving for leaves on high branches, and transmitted that characteristic to its descendants, so Nietzsche saw human intellectual ability rising by the same process. He therefore exhorts men, most particularly the best, to better themselves and their descendants by striving to accomplish great things, so that the superman may be created by this Lamarckian process. Indeed, according to Nietzsche, it is the duty of every human being, to the extent of his capacity, to sacrifice himself for the creation of the superman:

> I love those who . . . sacrifice themselves for the earth so that the earth may some day belong to the Overman.
>
> I love him who lives in order to know and who seeks knowledge so that the Overman may live. And thus he wills his own passing.
>
> I love him who works and invents in order to build a house for the Overman and to prepare for him the earth, the beasts, and the plants; for thus he wills his passing.[5]

Yet for all this, Nietzsche's superior man, who is to pave the way for and evolve into the superman, is not completely an altruist. Nietzsche visualizes human fulfillment, at least for the superior man, as lying in a continual process of self-improvement, self-renewal, and self-challenge. His aphorism, "The noble soul has reverence for itself" fitted Rand's thought perfectly; she nearly adopted it as the epigraph for *The Fountainhead*. Rand saw human fulfillment in much the same terms, though she extended it explicitly to all rational men, not just the strongest of the human race.

We should note that one of Nietzsche's most oft-stated themes is the necessity for continual challenge of one's intellectual substructure.

> Convictions are greater enemies of truth than lies.[6]
>
> The presupposition of every man of faith of any shade was that he could not be refuted. If the arguments against it prove to be too strong he could still take resource in belittling reason itself . . .[7]
>
> Are we under obligation to be true to our errors even when we realize that by doing so we do harm to our higher selves? . . . No, there is no law, no obligation of this kind; we must be traitors, must be disloyal, again and again must abandon our ideals.[8]

Here we may discern the root of Rand's "check your premises", as well as the realization that those who cannot justify their beliefs may reject reason rather than accept the truth.

More subtle but still detectable in its influence on Rand's work is Nietzsche's belief that intellectual and moral growth is inherently painful and indeed cruel. His view is that self-improvement involves not only effort but suffering—a sort of intellectual 'no pain, no gain' principle. This theme is recurrent through Nietzsche's work. To take just one example:

> Consider, that in his search for knowledge even the scholar, by forcing his intellect to know *against* the inclination of his mind, and often also against the wishes of his heart—that is to say No where he would prefer to affirm, love, and worship—is acting as an artist and transformer of cruelty . . . In every desire to know there is a drop of cruelty.[9]

Ayn Rand seems to have accepted and retained this idea herself. Rand's heroes are described in her early works explicitly as cruel; in her later works as "implacable". In spite of her emphasis on "the benevolent universe premise", she never completely lost the conviction that to grow and improve oneself is painful, that one must not be stopped by the pain, and that to assist others means, in a sense, to be cruel to them. Considered in this light, Henry Cameron's brusque treatment of Howard Roark; Francisco D'Anconia's deception of Dagny; and John Galt's cruelty toward both Dagny and Hank Rearden become more comprehensible.

In addition to these substantive contributions to the content of her thought, it is clear that Nietzsche also influenced Rand's literary style in several ways. Like Nietzsche, Rand wrote often in an aphoristic style. Like Nietzsche, she could be bitterly, even viciously polemical. The two writers are similar in their pleasure in shocking the reader, one announcing that "God is dead", the other proclaiming "the virtue of selfishness".

In her essay on the philosophical significance of the space program, 'Apollo and Dionysius', Rand invokes a metaphorical dichotomy taken directly from Nietzsche. But, unlike Nietzsche, who portrayed himself as a worshipper of Dionysius, Rand comes down on the side of the Apollonian worldview. Yet Ayn Rand, like Friedrich Nietzsche, was irreligious but not irreverent.

The subject of Nietzsche's influence on Rand could fill a book in itself; our discussion here merely scratches the surface. It is clear that Rand, as a philosopher and as a writer, derived much of her intellectual impulse from Nietzsche. Yet, as we shall see, she was in the end by no means his follower. Indeed, the significance of his influence was most marked in how she created Objectivism by struggling against it.

LITERARY INFLUENCES

No author, even one as independent as Ayn Rand, can completely avoid the influence of other writers. A number of sources contributed to Rand's literary technique and style. They constitute an eclectic collection.

The earliest inspiration for Rand's work came from the adventure melodramas she devoured as a young girl. Above all she was attracted by the heroes she found in these magazine serials: strong, resourceful, self-confident men who laughed at danger and were never at a loss for a way to deal with it. Her childhood experiments with writing concentrated on similar stories. But when she began serious work as an adult, the melodramatic hero was, mostly, suppressed; he did not return as a major factor until *Think Twice* and *Atlas Shrugged*.

Rand was of course familiar from her school days with the major Russian authors. She detested them for their sense of life, though admiring some (especially Dostoyevsky) for their powerful technique. She was more receptive to foreign authors, especially Schiller and Ibsen, and she loved Rostand's *Cyrano de Bergerac*. But the closest approach to her literary ideals was Victor Hugo.

Hugo, the leading Romantic of nineteenth-century literature, showed heroic men fighting for ideas. To portray this sort of struggle became Ayn Rand's own literary ambition. Hugo was her model, and in spite of her conscious effort to avoid imitation, the influence of Hugo is clear, especially in her early works.

But even Hugo was not quite *dramatic* enough for Rand's taste. Her work shows, almost from the beginning, a theatrical approach which appears to owe much to Henrik Ibsen. She must have thrilled indeed to *An Enemy of the People*. "The strongest man in the world is he who stands most alone", says Ibsen. "Every loneliness is a pinnacle", responds Rand.

Rand's predilection for paradox and her pleasure in surprising and shocking the reader probably owed much to the influence of O. Henry and Oscar Wilde. And, as we shall see, several authors may have contributed to specific plot devices or characters in her later novels. But overall, only Rand's earliest work is occasionally derivative; she established her literary independence far more quickly than most writers.

Rand's Early Fiction

Rand began writing in English shortly after her arrival in the United States. Her first efforts functioned primarily as exercises— apparently she made no effort to publish any of them—and they have little philosophical or intellectual content.

The earliest story by Ayn Rand that we have in print is 'The Husband I Bought', written in 1926. This seems to have been the first story Rand actually completed since her childhood efforts (she suspended her writing at age twelve, contenting herself with outlines and scenarios)—and it shows. It is so poorly constructed that it could not have been preceded by many serious efforts at fiction. Only the heroine, Irene, is fully characterized; the other characters, even her husband, receive only cursory attention. The plot is clearly improvised on a page-by-page basis; it seems unlikely that Rand knew, when she began the story, how it would end. She keeps things moving by the simple expedient of introducing new characters whenever needed. Irene needs a man to run away with—Voilà! A Mr. Gray appears from nowhere, wanting nothing more than to run away with her.

This story of a failed marriage is of more biographical than literary or philosophical interest. In view of its stylistic deficiencies Rand probably would not have preserved it had it not had a strong emotional significance to her. It is suggested by both Barbara Branden and Leonard Peikoff that in this story Rand worked out her emotional reaction to her first love, the Russian "Leo".

Though Peikoff attempts to place 'The Husband I Bought' into the context of Rand's work, the story is incapable of bearing much philosophical burden. Certainly the theme—loyalty to values—is one of the main unifying ideas of Rand's thought. Irene in dreary exile, kneeling before the portrait of her lost love, gives us a faint hint of Francisco D'Anconia's sad cabin in the forest. But the story, in the final analysis, is simply the maiden literary effort of a 21-year old girl who has had an unhappy love affair.

'Good Copy', written a year or so later, shows a very substantial improvement in technique. It is a humorous, almost slapstick account of a cub reporter's effort to stimulate his career by faking the kidnapping of an heiress. The stunt begins to backfire when the madcap heiress proves entirely too co-operative. The story is pure fun, of a type popular in the 1920s, and competently handled.

'Escort', a short-short written in 1929, is a conscious imitation of O. Henry, not nearly as good as that master's best but perhaps better than his worst.

Also written in 1929 was 'Her Second Career'. This is the first story that is recognizably written by Ayn Rand. The earlier works might have been produced by any beginning writer. But 'Her Second Career' shows the signs of Rand's mature fiction. First, there is the distinctive Randian 'gimmick': A Hollywood star is challenged to try starting over again at the bottom, to prove that her success is due to talent rather than luck or pull. Then, there are typical Randian heroes, the writer Winston Ayers and the aspiring actress Hedy Leland. The ironic twists of the plot are characteristic of the mature Rand.

And, an important sign of progress, Rand is now writing about reality. The settings of her earlier stories, though ordinary, are imaginary; Rand had no more direct knowledge of small-town 'society' or the newspaper business than she did of the African veldt. But the Hollywood milieu of 'Her Second Career' is unquestionably grounded in the personal experience of the author. Rand is now writing as an adult for the first time, drawing on experience rather than fantasy. Her description of the trials of aspiring actresses—including the petty indignities of the casting office and the not-so-petty indignities of the casting couch—has a gritty realism that adds impact to the story.

The story carries a limited but significant message. Rand indicts Hollywood for lacking the courage to develop new ideas, new stories, and new faces. She portrays effectively the movie industry herd phenomenon, with studio executives, each attempting to follow all the others, afraid to take the smallest chance on innovation.

RED PAWN

In 1930 Rand began work on her first novel, *We the Living*. A year later she interrupted the project to write a movie scenario, *Red Pawn*. This was her first commercial work to be completed, and her first sale.

Comparing *Red Pawn* to 'Her Second Career' shows that Rand's improvement in technique had not only continued but accelerated. The scenario is clearly a sketch for *We the Living*; theme and plot are identical with those of the novel. A woman (Joan/Kira) becomes the mistress of a dedicated Communist (Kareyev/Andrei) in order to save the life of the man she loves (Michael/Leo). Unexpectedly she comes to admire, and even love, the man she deceives; he in turn learns, from her example, that he must renounce his faith in Communism. But in the end her loyalty is to her first and greater love.

The two stories differ in two important respects. *Red Pawn* takes place in a prison, a limitation that effectively provides dramatic unity for a film. In *We the Living*, Russia itself is the prison; the novel can handle the wider scope.

More interesting is the contrast between the dénouements of the two stories. In *Red Pawn*, Kareyev's renunciation saves Joan and Michael, and they escape to Japan and freedom. In *We the Living*, Andrei's renunciation is futile; Leo and Kira are doomed. Rand may have felt that a 'happy' ending was mandatory for the film treatment.

Red Pawn marks another quantum leap in Rand's skill as a writer. The integration of plot, theme, and symbol is superb; Rand clearly is already a master of the esoteric art of writing for film. The characters of Joan and Karayev are brilliantly drawn; the only deficiency is Michael. Rand fails to project him as an effective hero, so that Joan's obsessive dedication lacks some credibility. She faced the same problem in *We the Living*.

Penthouse Legend

In 1933 Rand again interrupted her work on *We the Living* to write her first stage play, *Penthouse Legend*, which is more commonly known by the name *Night of January Sixteenth*. The play has been published in at least three editions: the McKay edition, intended for amateur productions; the Longman-Greens edition; and the authorized edition, put out by World Publishing.

Rand claims in her introduction to the authorized edition that it is essentially unchanged from her original manuscript. One may wonder whether this is wholly true; her similar claim with respect to *We the Living* is demonstrably false, as we shall see. However, there seems to be little in the authorized edition which could not have been written by the Rand of the 1930s, though she may have done a little philosophical airbrushing. Certainly the text is far more authentic Rand than either of the other two editions. There is only one passage missing from the authorized edition which seems authentic. It occurs at the end of the Longman-Greens edition: In both of the play's alternate conclusions, whether the verdict is guilty or not guilty, the judge chews out the jury and strikes their names from the rolls. *That* has the hallmark on it!

Rand goes to great pains in her introduction to the authorized edition to emphasize her rejection of the criminal-as-hero and to downplay the Nietzchean aspects of the work. A tortuous and unconvincing explication of the idea of a "sense-of-life play" is invoked to explain away the play's obvious philosophical thrust. A Nietzschean theme is so central to *Penthouse Legend* that Rand could never have hoped to Bowdlerize it—she would have had to eviscerate the plot.

Penthouse Legend is dominated by a character who never appears on stage: Bjorn Faulkner. He is a classic Nietzschean superman, a colossus of finance who is literally 'beyond good and evil' ("Bjorn never thought of things as right or wrong. To him, it was only: you can or you can't. He always could." [p. 102]) His only value is power: his "whip over the world" (p. 122) and his ownership of Karen Andre.

Karen Andre is drawn with a sure hand and is a striking character even in the elite group of Rand's heroines. In her combination of competence and sexuality she prefigures Dagny

Taggart, and in her insolent defiance of morality she prefigures Dominique Francon. She is, of course, a consummate hero-worshipper. Rand's lifelong theme of loyalty to values forms the basis of the plot: Karen Andre allows herself to be tried for Faulkner's murder to help him escape with his loot—not knowing that he really is dead. Reinforcing the theme is the comparable loyalty of the gangster 'Guts' Regan to Karen.

The play is a powerful and eloquent plea for the Nietzschean world view. Its epigraph might be Milton's, "better to reign in hell than serve in heav'n". But in the end, the Nietzschean vision must conclude with tragedy. What would be a happy ending for Faulkner? What could be? To rule the world? What would he do with it? He would be revealed as chasing a goal that would be useless if achieved; so he cannot be allowed to achieve it. Even the lesser goal of getting away with his ten million dollars cannot be practical. Is this the triumph of Bjorn Faulkner— to hide in Buenos Aires and play with his mistress and his money? Faulkner cannot succeed *and remain a hero*—so he must fail and die.

Just look at what happens. This 'superman' gives away his master plot by carelessly telling an underling too much. As Faulkner tries to sneak away, he is easily tailed by an amateur sleuth. And, finally, he is out-shot in a gunfight with a wealthy philanthropist. Poor Karen! Her hero not only dies, he dies ignominiously; he is not only murdered, he is humiliated.

On a technical level, the play is a skillfully constructed drama with a beautiful gimmick and extremely strong characters. Its only defect is Rand's peculiar inability to write an effective mystery plot without leaving holes. There are just too many problems with the prosecution's case: If the drunken man wasn't 'Lefty' O'Toole, who was he and what was he doing there? How did Karen Andre manage to throw Faulkner over a parapet? Why was no ballistics evidence presented?

Rand's stated theme in *Penthouse Legend* is, in effect, envy. Why are the great hated? Why do people gloat over the fall of the successful? Though she may well have started out with this theme in mind, the story apparently took on a mind of its own (as often happens) and the true theme ends up somewhat different:

Do we prefer conventional morality, even though its advocates are hypocrites—or downright fraud, open and unashamed?

The play, as *The Night of January Sixteenth*, had a moderate success on Broadway. Rand, like any writer for the stage, found that actually staging a play is a frustrating process of argument and compromise. In view of her hatred of compromise, and the philosophical chasm between author and director, it is not surprising that she found the entire process extremely unpleasant. Though she later wrote two more plays, neither made it to the stage—partly, perhaps, because she did not want to run the gantlet again. Exhausted from her struggle over *The Night of January Sixteenth*, and disgusted by the outcome, she resumed work on her first novel.

WE THE LIVING

Purely in terms of literary technique, *We the Living* is an absolutely extraordinary first novel. That a beginning writer, working in a language not her own, could produce a book so complex, subtle, skillfully structured, and emotionally powerful, and in the process deal with important philosophical and political themes in an original manner, marks her at once as a genius.

We the Living resembles most first novels in having strong elements of autobiography. Kira Argounova, like Ayn Rand, is the daughter of a Russian businessman; like Rand, she is a college student under the Soviet regime; like Rand, she works as a tour guide in a Bolshevik museum for a while. The details of life in the USSR in the 1920s, from the omnipresent melody of "John Gray" to pumping up the Primus stove, are impressed on the reader vividly in a way possible only to an author who has lived through the experience.

On its most superficial level, *We the Living* is a powerful political novel. "Tell them that Russia is a vast prison, and that we are all dying slowly," begged a young man as Rand prepared to leave the USSR. And Rand does so, depicting a totalitarian society with a painful, immediate realism.

On the next level, Rand deals with the theme that haunted her and drove her all her life: How does the heroic person survive in an evil society? In this book, she cannot even begin to develop a solution to this conundrum. Her heroes are destroyed, and only Kira's last smile hints that something better is possible.

On still a deeper level, the book is organized around another of Rand's universal themes: loyalty to values. This is the source, in fact, of the novel's plot.

For the book's heroine, Kira Argounova, there is, essentially, a single value: her love for the aristocrat Leo Kovalensky. Her attitude toward this value is very simple, and very characteristic of Rand: price no object.

THE THEME

With her typical ingenuity, Rand bases her plot on an ancient, hackneyed device—and gives it a new twist. A woman, to save the life of the man she loves, is forced to become the mistress of another man. As Nathaniel Branden has pointed out, this ancient cliché provides the plot for *Tosca* and many other stories. Rand's twist is that the other man, Andrei Taganov, is not the one who forces the heroine into his bed; indeed, he does not even know her motive but sincerely believes that she loves him. Nor is he despicable; Kira likes him and increasingly admires him.

The plot is shrewdly designed to give Rand the opportunity to build tension and develop a dramatic climax. Like any woman with two lovers, Kira is faced with the ever-more-difficult task of keeping them both in ignorance. The looming threat of discovery underlies the entire story like a pedal point as sub-plots develop on the upper stave.

Like most first novels, *We the Living* shows some derivative traits. The book owes much of its style and structure to techniques Rand had learned from Victor Hugo. In particular, Rand's narrative structure is in many ways parallel to that of *Ninety-Three*. Like Hugo's novel, *We the Living* has a plot based on a complex love-hate relationship between three primary characters, set against a background of revolution. In both books, the theme involves a conflict between the political beliefs and the personal moral values of the protagonists. And both novels climax with a series of intense personal confrontations between the three heroes.

TRIO FOR HEROES

Kira Argounova bears little resemblance to the corresponding character in *Red Pawn*. Joan is a mature, sophisticated woman; Kira is a naive girl, 18 as the novel begins. She is perhaps the least effectual of Rand's heroines. Her one positive accomplishment in the entire book is saving Leo from death from tuberculosis. For the rest, in spite of all her courage and determination, her life is one failure after another.

Kira's loyalty to values is expressed primarily in her love for Leo Kovalensky. Though Rand equips her with a career ambition—to become an engineer—it obviously does not dominate her as it would a later engineer/heroine, Dagny Taggart.[10] When Kira becomes involved in her love affair with Leo she finds her classes boring and cuts them. When a communist purge expels her from the university and her career plans are ruined, she is by no means crushed. One cannot help but suspect that her interest in engineering is an artificial part of her characterization, tacked on by Rand to make her more 'unconventional'.

It is Kira's love for Leo that is her driving force. Her behavior in this love affair shows Rand at her most typical. Kira meets Leo by allowing herself to be taken for a prostitute. When her family are outraged by the relationship, she cuts ties with them without a moment's hesitation. She is prepared to face death or imprisonment for Leo's sake. She becomes the mistress of a GPU officer to save Leo's life. One could scarcely ask for a stronger embodiment of Rand's theory that the good person will do anything—"price no object"—in defense of his highest value. Many will find this more credible in the case of Kira, whose highest value is a man, than in the case of Dagny, whose highest value is a railroad. But Rand regards the cases as essentially equivalent.

Leo, however, is a hero who does not satisfy. Rand, a daughter of the Russian bourgeoisie, throughout her life retained an admiration for the aristocracy, or at least the aristocratic manner; it is still visible even in *Atlas Shrugged*. Leo Kovalensky, the aristocrat, is her first fully-formed hero. Handsome and cruel, born to carry a whip, he seems a good candidate for the Nietzschean superman. But already Rand is beginning to show just the whisper of a doubt. Leo has arrogance, and even courage; he does not hesitate to insult his tormentors to their faces. One feels that he would face a firing squad well; it would be his finest moment. Yet his courage, like his beauty, is of the delicate sort. Just as his godlike body is that of a consumptive, so his arrogant soul cracks easily under prolonged pressure.

Like another fictional Nietzschean, Dorian Gray, Leo maintains a handsome exterior while his character gradually corrodes. From an aristocrat he descends to being an ordinary student; from that to a black market operator; from that to a gigolo. Kira fights in vain to save him from corruption.

For, like his fellow superman Bjorn Faulkner, Leo has no real place in the world. Perhaps in the old Russia he might have found his métier applying the knout to his serfs. But once again Rand is compelled by loyalty to her art to the conclusion that the Nietzschean superman does not really belong on this earth. Having portrayed her ideal, she can find no place for him. When Leo is making large profits in the black market, he shows no desire to save the money to escape from Russia. He could do no better anywhere else.

Andrei Taganov, too, shows the earmarks of a character who has escaped his author's hands and taken on a life of his own. In many ways he steals the show. Rand had a brilliant idea in making her villain/hero a communist—and not just a communist but a Chekist. But the logic of her plot and theme resulted in development of a character who, in the end, overshadows her intended hero. Taganov is an authentic hero, a real soldier, a man of strict integrity and true courage. Leo Kovalensky, the son of a White admiral, did not carry arms in the Civil War. He cuts a rather poor figure in comparison to Taganov.

Andrei in the end is much closer to Kira than Leo is. He too has a value to pursue: communism. It is this which draws them together initially; though their values are antithetical, they are alike in having a loyalty to a supreme value. But as the true face of communism appears, Andrei, like Kira, finds his idol turning to corruption before his eyes. Though he transfers his loyalty to Kira, she is irrevocably Leo's.

A CINEMATIC STYLE

As in plot, so also in style does *We the Living* closely follow Hugo. Though Rand made a conscious effort to avoid imitating Hugo, she nonetheless ended up adopting many of his devices, especially in her descriptive passages—her essay on St. Petersburg could easily have come directly from Hugo's pen—and in her carefully positioned flashbacks. She also borrowed from Hugo the use of short, sometimes one-sentence paragraphs to provide impact. Indeed, she continued to use this technique throughout her fiction career, though not so heavily; in her 1958 revision of *We the Living* she substantially reduced the use of this device. Again copied from Hugo is sharp, significant dialogue very much in the French style.

However, perhaps the most striking aspect of the novel's style is its powerful visual element. Even more than her other works, *We the Living* shows the influence of Rand's experience as a Hollywood screenwriter. Andrei's suicide scene has already been mentioned, but the novel is full of other scenes which are visually dramatic—not merely 'theatrical' but specifically cinematic. The student meeting with its green and red caps and the *Internationale* competing with the traditional student song was custom-tailored for the silver screen. Kira's pickup of Leo in a red-light district was ready without modification for a Griffith or Welles or Lang. And the book's climax could hardly be bettered for suitability for the cinema.

It is not surprising that Italian director Gofredo Alessandrini was driven to film the story during World War II. Thanks to the efforts of Henry and Erika Holzer, this superb movie is now available on videotape. The film is strikingly faithful to the novel— though, unlike the movie of *The Fountainhead*, Rand had nothing to do with the production. The close resemblance between the film and the novel can only be ascribed to the natural cinematic character of the latter.

THE CHANGES

We the Living was published in 1936 and quickly went out of print. After the success of *Atlas Shrugged* the earlier novel was revived, with revisions by Rand, in 1959. Rand, in her introduction to the revised version, asserted that she merely cleaned up grammar and awkward wording: "In brief, all the changes are merely editorial line-changes." This is somewhat less than true.

One must not exaggerate the importance of Rand's revisions. They are not extensive, and most of them are minor. As previously mentioned, some choppy paragraphs are consolidated. One character's style of speech is changed. A rather gory description of Bolshevik atrocities is expunged (p. 455). Some changes are merely puzzling: an allusion to Kira's virginity is removed (p. 141); Leo quotes Spinoza rather than Kant (p. 156).

One short passage is excised in which Leo is described as "not a lover, but a slave owner", and Kira longs to be under his whip. Throughout her fiction Rand presents a model of female sexual submission that sometimes seems to border on masochism; perhaps she decided this particular passage went a bit too far.

However, two passages in the first edition have been modified in a way which clearly shows an intent to expurgate Nietzschean ideas. Both occur (pp. 92–95) in an argument between Kira and Andrei shortly after they have first met. In the first passage, Kira, speaking of communism, says (starting out with a typical Randian cliché-reversal):

> "I loathe your ideals. I admire your methods. If one believes one's right, one shouldn't wait to convince millions of fools, one might just as well force them. Except that I don't know, however, whether I'd include blood in my methods."
>
> "Why not? Anyone can sacrifice his own life for an idea. How many know the devotion that makes you capable of sacrificing other lives? Horrible, isn't it?"
>
> "Not at all. Admirable. If you're right. But are you right?"

Rand removes this entire passage; in the revised edition. Kira says merely, "I loathe your ideals,"

A few paragraphs further on, Kira becomes brutally explicit:

> "Don't you know," he asked, "that we can't sacrifice millions for the sake of the few?"
>
> "You can! You must. When those few are the best. Deny the best its right to the top—and you have no best left. What are your masses but mud to be ground underfoot, fuel to be burned for those who deserve it? What is the people but millions of puny, shrivelled, helpless souls that have no thoughts of their own, no dreams of their own, no will of their own, who eat and sleep and chew helplessly the words others put into their mildewed brains? And for those you would sacrifice the few who know life, who *are* life? I loathe your ideals because I know no worse injustice than justice for all. Because

men are not born equal and I don't see why one should want to make them equal. And because I loathe most of them."

Here is the revised version:

> "Don't you know," he asked, "that we can't sacrifice millions for the sake of the few?"
> "Can you sacrifice the few? When those few are the best? Deny the best its right to the top—and you have no best left. What are your masses but millions of dull, shrivelled, stagnant souls that have no thoughts of their own, no dreams of their own, no will of their own, who eat and sleep and chew helplessly the words others put into their brains? And for those you would sacrifice the few who know life, who *are* life? I loathe your ideals because I know no worse injustice than the giving of the undeserved. Because men are not equal in ability and one can't treat them as if they were. And because I loathe most of them."

These passages display Andrei Taganov as a committed and consistent communist. His goal, as he states elsewhere in the argument, is to raise the masses to his own level. Any means, including massive bloodshed, is justified by this end; but he finds the necessary killing horrible.

Kira counters, in the original passages, with a classical Nietzschean point of view. The masses are worthless; they are to be exploited, or even destroyed, for the sake of the "best". She personally dislikes bloodshed, but she admires those who are not limited by what she seems to regard as her overfastidiousness.

These passages, unlike the revised versions, are perfectly in character for Kira. They are consistent with her thought and speech and behavior throughout the book. The revised passage, on the other hand, is anachronistic and—in terms of Kira's personal style—out of character. Nowhere else in the book does she speak about superior abilities or the giving of the undeserved. Though she might well agree with such sentiments, Kira Argounova simply does not think in those terms. They represent the Rand of the 1950s, not the Rand of the 1930s; it is Dagny Taggart speaking, not Kira Argounova.

What may we conclude? We certainly cannot accept Rand's assertion that her revision "reworded the sentences and clarified their meaning". Her meaning was perfectly clear in the original. Kira Argounova, speaking for Rand, adopts in the most explicit terms possible the ethical position of Friedrich Nietzsche.

But it must be realized that Rand already was showing signs of challenging this position. Kira's reluctance to resort to violence is a portent. And a few sentences later she says that she does not want to fight for or against the people, she wants to be left alone to live. This clearly foreshadows the Objectivist position.

THE FAILURE OF NIETZSCHE

We the Living is the neglected stepchild of Rand's novels. This is partly due, no doubt, to the fact that it is less didactic and carries less philosophical content than her later works. Further, the story is extremely depressing; one may, as I do, admire the literary technique while feeling little inclination to reread the book for pleasure. However, it is likely that *We the Living* receives less than its due because of its embarrassing and disturbing Nietzschean themes, which are still evident even in the revised version. Yet to any serious student of Rand's work, this book is an essential starting point.

With *We the Living* Rand reached complete maturity as a writer. Through her fiction she had begun to grapple seriously with ethical issues. And, as a direct result, she began to develop the ideas which were to grow into Objectivism.

It is easy to criticize Rand for having once held to ethical precepts which are invalid, even evil. It is still easier to criticize her for lying about these beliefs in later life. Yet these ideas provided a necessary foundation for the edifice that she was later to erect. Just as Aristotle taught her logic and metaphysics, so Nietzsche provided Rand with the root of her sense of life, the emphasis on achievement, on aspiration, on pursuing supremely important values. It is to her credit that she was able to clear away the debris of his ethical monstrosities and keep what was good as she built Objectivism.

With the completion of *We the Living* Rand entered a period of philosophical transition. Ayn Rand was never a person who changed her mind easily, and the repudiation of her Nietzschean beliefs must have involved a formidable internal struggle. Out of this struggle grew the work which made her famous— *The Fountainhead*.

4 | THE TRANSITION PERIOD

R and's career in America was close to its nadir in 1934. *We the Living* could not find a publisher; *Penthouse Legend* could not find a producer. With her savings running out, her husband unable to find work, her adopted country deep in the Great Depression, Rand might have been excused had she given way to despair.

During this period of stress—and perhaps in some way as a result of her emotional turmoil—Rand took the first decisive steps away from Nietzsche. Unfortunately, it is difficult to follow her progress in this critical transition; we only know that somehow, during the next three years, she renounced the Nietzschean superman in favor of Howard Roark.

Some evidence of Rand's thinking during this period is available from two plays: *Ideal* and *Think Twice*.

THE ENIGMA OF *IDEAL*

In all of Rand's output, there is no work which presents so many problems to the analyst as *Ideal*. Almost everything else she wrote is absolutely pellucid; the reader need never be in doubt as to what she is saying and what she means. *Ideal* provides a striking contrast.

The basic story is straightforward enough. Kay Gonda, a much-worshipped movie star, disappears; she is suspected of murder. We see her approach, one by one, a series of people who have written adoring fan letters, and ask for asylum. Each one fails her. A left-wing writer tries to sell her out for the reward money; an artist who has painted her again and again cannot even recognize her in the flesh; a preacher exhorts her to confess. All those who idolized her fail, when challenged, to value their ideal—except for Johnnie Dawes, an unemployed drifter. To clear her of suspicion, he confesses falsely to the murder of which she is accused, then commits suicide. In the final scene, we learn that Kay Gonda was innocent of the 'murder'; she framed herself for the crime, in order to discover the reaction of her fans.

Ideal was initially written as a novelette, and later transformed into a two-act play; it was never produced. The story (as Rand herself recognized[1]) would have been better left as a novelette; the narrative is simply not well suited to the stage, though Rand achieved a number of well-crafted dramatic touches. But it is not primarily literary problems that the play poses.

The direct interpretation of *Ideal* is straightforward. When put to the test, Gonda's admirers betray their professed ideal. On this level, the story is a condemnation of the almost universal lack of integrity, and the theme is very efficiently handled. As always, Rand retains her theme of loyalty to values.

The problem arises with the motivation of the two principle characters, Gonda and Dawes. Why does she go to such lengths to search for integrity? How could a person like Dawes possess that integrity?

Rand's difficulty in expressing these critical factors in the story indicates the deep-seated questioning of her own values while she was writing it. She was groping for an entirely new view of life at this time. Had *Ideal* been written a couple of years earlier it would likely have had a very different ending; perhaps with a disillusioned Kay Gonda staggering into a police station to give herself up and face trial and execution. In a Nietzschean world there is no integrity to be found in the masses, and the superman—or superwoman—whose spiritual fuel 'runs dry' is doomed.

For this is Gonda's motive: she creates for her fans an ideal world, an ideal person; but who is to be her ideal? She gives them the courage to face life; but who is to give her courage? She must know; is she the only person on earth who still pursues an ideal with integrity, who has not given up her childhood dreams? Is integrity possible at all? Like Nietzsche's Zarathustra, she comes down from her lonely pinnacle to the world of men—only to be disappointed.

Leonard Peikoff points out that Gonda, like Dominique in *The Fountainhead*, and like Rand herself ("in a bad mood"), suffers from an idealistic alienation from the world. In this sense, *Ideal* may be considered a first sketch for *The Fountainhead*. But Peikoff unjustly classes Gonda below Dominique. For, as we shall see, Dominique has already despaired as *The Fountainhead* begins; convinced that her ideal is unattainable, she acts as a destroyer. Kay Gonda, on the other hand, has not given up. She is desperate but not despairing. And in the end she does find—in a way—the integrity she is seeking.

But this brings us to the character of Johnnie Dawes, a most unlikely Rand hero. Physically he fits the bill: tall, a gaunt face, a hard mouth and steady eyes. But what else is there? A college graduate (with an unspecified major), he fails to hold even the job of a bellhop or a waiter. He shows no purpose in life; he is unable to live in the world as it is, but lacks the resolution to change it. "I'm nothing," is his description of himself.

His one value is his ideal, Kay Gonda. His one redeeming trait is his determination to act to protect his ideal. And to save her he dies, as he tells us, "perfectly happy."

In actual fact, Johnnie's action is unnecessary. Gonda is innocent—indeed, the 'murder' never even happened—and she is in no danger. But when her press agent condemns her for allowing Johnnie to die, she replies, "That, Mick, was the kindest thing I have ever done." For, as she has realized, his death was a kindness; Johnnie Dawes had no future.

Yet, in another way, Johnnie's death does save Gonda's life. This ultimate testimony to the possibility of human integrity gives her the conviction to go on living.

As Kay Gonda surveys her fans, Rand compares different responses to the disillusionment of childhood ideals—as a means, perhaps, of confronting the crisis in her own ideals. George Perkins, the first fan, simply gives them up for a life of pure convention. Chuck Fink, the leftist, holds to his ideals even when he learns that they are actually evil, and thus descends into an amoral viciousness. Dwight Langley, the artist, holds to an ideal but considers it impossible of achievement on earth. Claude Hix, the preacher, goes even farther; if an ideal should appear on earth rather than in heaven, it must be sacrificed. The playboy, Esterhazy, finds that he cannot climb out of the quicksand of cynicism which he so casually entered.

But Johnnie Dawes is no hero, either. He has retained a child's dedication to an ideal, but at the price of remaining a child. He has an ideal, he is faithful to her, he knows that he must not merely admire but act. He has a child's piercing emotional insight and empathy. But he has despaired—not of the world, but of himself. He too has betrayed his ideal—by refusing to grow up.

We now see the dramatic unity in the play's conclusion. Kay Gonda is not, after all, revitalized at the end. We see her exhausted, indifferent, almost bitter. She has not found what she wanted; but she has found, in the most direct possible way, that she must live. She is loyal to her ideal; Johnnie Dawes' escape is not for her. She has found the one person in the world with integrity: herself. And that integrity will not let her quit.

Ideal seems to have served Rand as a preliminary study in which she experimented with the theme of treason to values. Presently we shall see how this germ of an idea blossomed into the extraordinary plot of *The Fountainhead*.

THINK TWICE

While writing *The Fountainhead*, Rand several times interrupted her work on the novel to complete smaller projects—primarily in the hope of developing some income. *Think Twice*, a two-act play written in 1939, was one of these projects. The play prefigures *Atlas Shrugged* in certain respects—notably in its combination of philosophical and mystery elements, and in its scientist hero. However, it appears to have functioned primarily as a sketch for *The Fountainhead*—in particular, for the character of Ellsworth Toohey. Walter Breckenridge, the villain of *Think Twice*, is clearly a primitive, unfinished version of Toohey, her most complex and fascinating badman.

Breckenridge, like Toohey, is a power-luster acting in the guise of a humanitarian, who controls his victims by 'helping' them.

This provides the root of the play's mystery element. On his birthday Breckenridge invites his victims to his new house, and uses the occasion to torment them with a sophisticated but nonetheless vicious sadism. It is hardly surprising that he is murdered before the first act ends.

As a mystery, the play fails; one can easily deduce the murderer, and not in the way Rand suggested either.[2] However, it is an exciting and entertaining drama. It richly merits production, and it is a pity that it never made it to the stage.

As a sketch for the character of Toohey, Breckenridge is only a skeleton. Indeed, his characterization, in the final analysis, is the play's major weakness. Breckenridge has too little to say for himself, and his final confrontation with his murderer is thereby lacking in the dramatic tension it deserves. It seems likely that Rand learned from this sketch that Toohey must be a more eloquent villain, more self-consciously evil—though, as we will see, this introduced new problems.

On the other hand, as a philosophical drama *Think Twice* is highly effective. In a marvelous piece of integrated symbolism, Rand dates the play on July Third and Fourth, with Independence Day for Breckenridge's slaves announced by fireworks—climaxed by the pistol shot which kills him. Rand exercises brilliantly her talent for making a philosophical theme concrete.

The hero of *Think Twice*, Steve Ingalls, is clearly in the Objectivist rather than the Nietzschean mold—indeed, he seems more similar to John Galt than to Howard Roark. One must keep in mind, however, that the play was revised as late as the 1950s, while Rand was writing *Atlas Shrugged*; the published version may not give us an accurate vision of her thinking at the time the play was originally written.

Writing these two plays clearly gave Rand a chance to develop key themes and characters which would appear in *The Fountainhead*. She now felt ready to tackle her masterwork, the novel she'd wanted to write all her life, the story of her ideal, her ultimate hero.

THE FOUNTAINHEAD

Judged purely as a piece of literature, *The Fountainhead* is Ayn Rand's best work. Although it lacks the enormous philosophical scope and the intricate multi-level organization of plot and theme that we find in *Atlas Shrugged*, the earlier book presents a fascinating and subtle interplay of ethical and psychological themes.

On one level, *The Fountainhead* is a treatment of Rand's professed theme: the ideal man, Howard Roark. She set out initially to portray the ideal man. It is no coincidence, one may suspect, that the book begins and ends with the words, "Howard Roark".

But she did not get far into the construction of the novel before encountering two serious problems. First, she simply was not ready to portray the ideal man; her ideas, her ideals, were in a state of flux at that time and she was far from having developed them sufficiently to accomplish her self-assigned task.

Second, from the point of view of literary technique, problems arise in writing a story about an 'ideal' person. To use a central character who is morally perfect makes it difficult to center the story on an internal moral conflict. Adopting a hero who has no psychological problems rules out centering the story on psychological conflict. Thus when we encounter an 'ideal' hero, the story usually involves a basic dilemma of some less fundamental sort, such as a physical challenge.

Rand resolved this problem in *The Fountainhead* by removing Roark from the lead role. In the novel as it exists, Roark is 'off stage' for over half of the book. Instead, Dominique Francon becomes the real protagonist. The plot-theme of the book now becomes something different: 'How would imperfect people react to the ideal man?' This makes it possible to center the plot on a moral conflict within Dominique—and, later in the book, Gail Wynand.

For, on this level, *The Fountainhead* is a novel about the sin of despair. Though Rand would no doubt have been horrified to hear it thus described, the book has a theme prominent in Christian theology. Hope (as in "faith, hope, and charity") is a virtue in Christian doctrine because its antithesis, despair, leads one to feel that it is permissible to sin. If evil is destined to inevitable triumph, why struggle to achieve virtue? This is precisely the fundamental premise of Dominique and Wynand. Having despaired, not believing that good can triumph, they permit themselves to do evil. Wynand uses his 'power' to exalt the banal in human existence, and to crush men who show signs of integrity. Dominique wastes her talents and, like Wynand, leaves a trail of agony behind her, as she does her best to destroy that which she most values, from statues, to Roark, to her own soul.

On still another level, *The Fountainhead* deals with the twin issues of independence and integrity. Rand's unification of these two virtues is not sufficiently appreciated. One of her objectives in the novel is to show that independence, in the end, must mean intellectual independence. The man who allows others to tell him what to think, thereby allows others to tell him what to do. Rand provides numerous examples of this principle, culminating in the illuminating scene where Peter Keating is reduced to abject slavery by Ellsworth Toohey. Rand goes on to show that integrity can exist only in the man who possesses intellectual independence. For the 'second-hander', dependent on others for his beliefs, can never resist their sway.

On still another level, Rand in *The Fountainhead* returns to her perennial theme: How can the good man live in an evil society? As we shall see, she still could not find a satisfactory answer to this riddle.

THE BREAK WITH NIETZSCHE

But above all, *The Fountainhead* is Ayn Rand's explicit and final renunciation of the morality of Friedrich Nietzsche. Rand clearly intended this theme and she sets up the conflict quite explicitly early in the novel. When Henry Cameron retires, passing on the torch to Roark, he tells him that, of all the evil in the world, Gail Wynand represents what he has to fight. And in fact, one might well interpret the story as an allegorical struggle between Roark—representing, in a primitive form, Objectivist morality—and Wynand, representing Nietzschean morality—for the soul of Dominique—Rand's alter ego.

For Wynand is indeed the very incarnation of the Nietzschean superman. He is in the tradition of Rand's youthful whip-wielding aristocratic heroes. Though he starts out as a slum boy, both of his parents are suggested to have been of 'good family'; his father's nickname, "the Duke", explicitly evokes aristocracy. Wynand rises without help, solely by means of his unique ability and his iron determination. Not for him the 'slave morality';

he regards himself as 'beyond good and evil'. With an explicit childhood decision he devotes his life to the pursuit of power.

Roark, by contrast, is the prototype of the Objectivist hero. It is very clear from a reading of Rand's out-takes from *The Fountainhead* (see *The Early Ayn Rand*) that her vision of Roark was still evolving as she wrote the novel. The Roark who was excised, particularly in the 'Vesta Dunning' passages, retains vestiges of the superman: cruelty, violence, aloofness. The Roark who remains evolves still more during the story. As he matures (and as Rand matured), Roark becomes more emotionally open, more introspective, more willing to relate to, and value, other people.

Dominique Francon, like Rand's other heroines, is an expression of Rand's own personality. Like Rand, she struggles with the problem of existence in a world hostile to rationality. Rand described Dominique as "myself in a bad mood". But Dominique is this and much more; her extraordinarily complex and subtle psychology enriches the novel.

To paraphrase one of Rand's favorite quotations from Aristotle, one might describe Dominique as a neurotic—not as neurotics are, but as they should be. She is a fundamentally rational and even heroic person, driven over the edge by the devastating pressure of an irrational society. At the root of her personality is a moral flaw: despair. She has, quite explicitly, given up on life. She knows what is good—and she 'knows' that the good has no chance. Building on this single thesis, Rand constructs a complex and consistent personality. Her psychological insight is impressive on its own terms, and astounding when one realizes the extent to which she must have confronted her own internal conflicts to develop such an analysis.

At the beginning of the novel, we see Dominique living solely for amusement—the amusement of teasing and tormenting the people she despises. She has intentionally subjected herself to total emotional repression. When she finds a statuette that she loves, she destroys it—not, as she tells Alvah Scarrett, so that nobody else will see it, but so that she herself will not see it—because she cannot allow herself to feel what it makes her feel. After making a promising start as a journalist, she sabotages her own career for fear that she might come to enjoy it too much. She has no friends; she cares nothing for her father; when men embrace her, she feels no desire, nor even revulsion.

The fundamental, thematic conflict in the novel arises from the simple fact that for a woman of Dominique's intense life-force, this emotional repression is unsustainable. The crack in her armor is Howard Roark. This is the man who is her proper mate, a fitting hero. But how can she respond to him? Later in the story, Wynand, who faces the same problem, says that love could come to him only in a twisted form. In the same way, Roark can come to Dominique only as a 'rapist'.

The famous 'quarry sequence' shows Rand's literary technique at its best. Dominique's struggle to maintain—or rather to restore—her repression is described with masterful psychological insight. Roark, naive though he is at this stage, cannot but recognize her need: "Pressure is a powerful factor. It leads to consequences which, once started, cannot be controlled." It certainly does!

In the wake of her encounter with Roark, Dominique is compelled to follow the logic of her psychological premises. She must, of course, destroy him—not, as she says, to save him from the world's corruption, but to allow her to restore her repression. But she also realizes that she is faced with a further task: she must destroy not just Roark but herself. If values have no chance in the world, then her only value—her own integrity—is itself a threat to her. Ultimately she must degrade herself. This she attempts, first by marrying Peter Keating, then by agreeing to be rented (and later sold) to Gail Wynand.

And yet, she cannot succeed. Repeatedly she breaks down—she defends Roark at the Stoddard Temple trial; she warns Peter Keating not to marry her; she tries to torture Wynand, and then to save him from Toohey.

Paradoxically, it is by seeking her deepest degradation that Dominique finds the way out of her morass. Voluntarily prostituting herself for the benefit of a man she despises, she encounters Gail Wynand.[3] These two are similar in what they value, and in their treason to those values. It is this similarity which draws them to each other. But their marriage traps both of them into confrontation with their fundamental error. Intellectually, Dominique cannot avoid seeing, exposed at close range, Wynand's treason to his own values—and he cannot avoid seeing hers. Emotionally, Dominique cannot avoid responding to Wynand—just as he cannot make of her just another mistress to be toyed with and discarded. But by opening themselves to such emotions they both begin to experience the break-up of their defensive repression.

The return of Howard Roark from exile at just this point completely upsets the already tottering emotional balance of Dominique and Wynand. Unable to return to their repressed state, they are drawn by Roark back to reality, to the necessity of values and the need to fight for them.

The plot-climax, the dynamiting of Cortlandt Homes, serves to bring to a crisis Dominique's internal conflict as well as Wynand's. Finally they renounce their treason and fight together for Howard Roark and the values he represents. But their crime—treason, the deepest and vilest of crimes, which dooms one to freeze in the ninth circle of hell—cannot be expiated so easily. Dominique, in an ecstasy of self-mutilation that virtually compels comparison to religious penitence and mortification, nearly kills herself. Wynand fares even worse; he closes the *Banner* and actually does kill himself.[4]

Why is Dominique redeemed but not Wynand? Essentially, because of Roark. Dominique, a woman, can re-center her values on the man she worships. This gives her a base on which to rebuild her life. But Wynand, having dedicated his life to power, has nothing left when he sees that power is worse than worthless. The superman, with his 'morality of masters', is revealed to be the slave of the masses he despises. His dream of a Wynand Building becomes a mockery and a reproach; he is too old to go back to Hell's Kitchen and start from scratch. For Gail Wynand, as for Johnnie Dawes, there is only one way out, only one way he can serve the ideal he recognizes.

A TRADITIONAL ANTITHESIS

Part of the nineteenth-century literary tradition in which Rand was steeped was the novel based on contrast of antitheses. We see this in such titles as *Sense and Sensibility*, *Crime and Punishment*, *War and Peace*. Rand begins *The Fountainhead* by setting up a comparison of this type: the man of independent thought, Howard Roark, and the intellectual 'second-hander', Peter Keating. This effective literary device, by contrasting the two personalities and society's reaction to them, helps to clarify and define Roark's personal character.

Those who condemn Rand for creating only 'black and white' characters ought to be surprised and pleased by Peter Keating. He is as 'gray' as they could ask for. Keating is a man of no small ability; critics who portray him as an incompetent are missing Rand's point. Keating has the intellectual potential to become a first-rate artist—his original ambition—or even a first-rate architect. But his failure to establish independence arrests the development of his abilities. Achievement and ability, like all other values, depend on independence.

Keating is a sort of amateur—or let us say, small-time, petty—Gail Wynand. While congratulating himself on his manipulation of other people, he fails to notice that it is he who is being pushed around. He allows himself to be talked out of the career he wants, of the wife he wants, of everything that might bring him satisfaction in life.[5] In the end he has nothing to show for his life, in spite of—indeed, because of—all the 'practical' compromises he has made.

THE IMPOSSIBLE VILLAIN

Rand's depiction of Peter Keating is a classic of psychological insight. He perfectly fulfills his literary role as a foil for Roark. But he cannot for a moment be visualized as the villain of the piece. That role must go to the inimitable Ellsworth Toohey.

Like his embryonic precursor, Walter Breckenridge, Toohey persuades young people to forsake the careers they love, thus depriving them of joy in their work. But compared to Toohey, Breckenridge is a beginner. Toohey is a master criminal, a Moriarty of the mind. He uses a whole arsenal of techniques to destroy his victims. He advises them to indulge in casual sex—and avoid serious romance. He presses Peter Keating to marry for prestige and professional advancement instead of love. He advocates compromise of moral principles as not only unavoidable but desirable. He uses humor as a weapon to ridicule and degrade anything good. He attacks integrity, independence, and reason.

Toohey, the quintessential Randian villain, seems to be a caricature of her philosophical arch-enemy, Immanuel Kant. If one wishes to look at the novel in allegorical terms, one might say that

Rand has realized that Nietzsche's approach, as exemplified by Gail Wynand, is unable to deal with Kant/Toohey; it is only Objectivism, as embodied in Howard Roark, that can defeat him.

But Rand pays a price for making Toohey such a perfect personification of evil. The character ultimately loses psychological reality: One meets Peter Keating every day, and one can imagine meeting Roark or Wynand, but one could never meet Ellsworth Toohey. The problem is that Toohey not only is evil, but knows that he is evil. He has no self-delusion in him. Nobody could function in reality on such a basis; in *Atlas Shrugged*, Rand makes James Taggart go mad on being confronted with his own evil. So Rand ends up using Toohey not really as a character but as a personification of evil. He might best be compared to Goethe's Mephistopheles.

Western literature has long displayed a sort of fascination with the personification of evil, and what Toohey lacks in psychological realism he more than makes up as a brilliant specimen of demonology. He makes a tawdry, contemptible Satan, much more in the style of C.S. Lewis than of Milton or Goethe. But he is all the more effective a tempter for that.

INTELLECTUAL SNOBBERY

As she delineates Toohey's little games, Rand provides an analysis of one of the most common, and frustrating, con games of our century: intellectual snobbery. Today more than ever, what passes for high culture is dominated by those who pretend to admire the ridiculous, the incomprehensible, the disgusting, and sneer at those who 'can't understand'.

Any young person who has studied Heidegger; or seen Ionesco's 'plays'; or listened to the 'music' of John Cage; or looked at Andy Warhol's 'paintings'—has experienced that feeling of incredulous puzzlement: But this is nonsense! Can I really be expected to take this seriously?

In fact, of course, it is necessary for it to be nonsense; if it made sense, it could be evaluated. The essence of modern intellectual snobbery is the 'emperor's new clothes' approach. Teachers, critics, our self-appointed intellectual elite, make it quite clear to us that if we cannot see the superlative nature of this 'art'—why, it merely shows our ignorance, our lack of sophistication and insight. Of course, they go beyond the storybook emperor's tailors, who dressed their victim in nothing and called it fine garments. The modern tailors dress the emperor in garbage.

Rand brilliantly exposes this deception, and her portrait of Lois Cook, an emperor's tailor if there ever was one, provides some of the novel's most entertaining and illuminating scenes.

A SEAMLESS PATCHWORK

In the first draft of *The Fountainhead* the story focus on Howard Roark was stronger and more personal. Part of this narrative described Roark's first sexual experience, an affair with the aspiring actress Vesta Dunning, which ends when she sells out her ideals to get good parts. By the time Rand finished Part One of the book, technical problems were already apparent. When the publisher asked for cuts, she took advantage of the opportunity to eliminate Vesta and recast the structure of the novel.

By removing the 'Vesta Dunning' passages from *The Fountainhead* Rand effectively conceded her change of the novel's theme. Having dropped her original intention of centering the story on Roark, she had to tighten the story's focus on Dominique as the female protagonist; Vesta had to go. Much of the material removed had Roark on stage, so that the new focus of the story on Dominique was further enhanced.

The primary plot-line of *The Fountainhead* narrates Dominique's struggle with herself. Her internal conflict involves both a moral issue—treason to values—and a psychological issue—emotional repression. Rand intertwines these two strands skillfully to weave the basic thread of the plot.

In keeping with its paradoxically Christian theme, *The Fountainhead*'s primary plot is analogous to that of Dante's *Inferno*: The protagonist, having lost the right way, voluntarily enters Hell, confronting the meaning of evil and finally finding the way out at the very bottom. Dominique, in her downward progression, encounters successively more serious sins, from the venial offenses of Guy Francon, through Keating and Hopton

Stoddard and Lois Cook, until she is faced with her own crime in the person of Gail Wynand.

This, the 'new' plot, is spliced into Rand's 'old' plot so smoothly one scarcely notices the joining. The original story of the antithesis between Roark and Keating is arranged as contrary motion. In the first section of the book, we see Keating rise and Roark fall. In the last section, their roles are reversed. In between, the 'old' plot is more or less suspended and Dominique's Dantesque journey of self-discovery takes center stage.

The third strand of the story is, quite literally, a plot: Ellsworth Toohey's campaign to take control of the Wynand empire. This line of action serves several functions in the story, the most important of which is the development of the climax—the Cortlandt bombing and the Wynand strike struggle.

It will be seen that *The Fountainhead* is far more complex in structure than *We the Living*. Rand's ability to develop a multilevel plot structure and tie together several major story lines represents another advance from her earlier work. Her false start was corrected so skillfully one can scarcely see the repair lines.

ACQUITTAL UNSATISFACTORY

When it comes to Rand's lifelong dilemma—the survival of reason and heroic achievement in a hostile world—*The Fountainhead* fails to present a convincing solution. The novel, as we have seen, treats the issue of the sin of despair. Rand rejects despair, but she has no real answer yet. The book ends on a note of triumph, but Roark's vindication ultimately rests on faith. A jury of 'the common man' acquits Roark after hearing his courtroom speech in defense of individualism. This doubtless reflects Rand's experience as a soapbox orator during the Wendell Willkie campaign, which gave her an abiding respect for the commonsense rationality of the (literal) 'man in the street'. The same phenomenon is used in the scene of Rearden's trial in *Atlas Shrugged*. There, however, it becomes merely an incident, rather than a resolution. Rand by then recognized that the 'common man's' response to reason is temporary; when the influence of the rational hero is removed, the 'common man' returns to irrationality.

Thus, to the reader, Roark's acquittal fails to carry conviction.

However, *The Fountainhead* does at least give a hint of the solution that Rand will find in *Atlas Shrugged*. By renouncing Nietzsche she comes to the concept of the impotence of evil. Says Roark to Toohey, "But I don't think of you." This is the attitude that Rand's earlier characters aspire to, but cannot achieve. Howard Roark is an assertion that the heroic man can defeat the excruciating pressure of society by sheer grit. Unfortunately, in practice this tends to reduce to avoiding alienation by means of emotional repression—the trap into which Dominique and Wynand fall. So this answer did not satisfy Rand, and she returned to the problem in *Atlas Shrugged*. Ultimately she found her solution in the concept of the "sanction of the victim".

THE EMBRYO OF OBJECTIVISM

With Roark's courtroom speech at the climax of *The Fountainhead*, Rand decisively cuts her ties with Friedrich Nietzsche. The power-seeking 'superman' is explicitly classed with the altruist as merely another 'second-hander'. The true egoist, Rand has decided, is not the ruler but the creator. Morality is not a chain for slaves but the root of freedom.

But though Rand had finally crossed the border, she had not yet reached the capital of the terrain which was to become Objectivism. That became her next task.

Nonetheless, several of the basic ideas of Objectivism are explicated in *The Fountainhead*. Reliance on reason, not yet a major theme, is nonetheless clearly adopted. A related idea, the impotence of evil, is explicit in the novel. Roark's final speech is devoted primarily to the key concepts of creativity and self-generated action as the proper life for man. We can see the roots of the Objectivist ethics, but they are still unsupported. During the next 13 years Rand laid the groundwork in metaphysics and epistemology that would put the Objectivist ethics on a firm footing.

ANTHEM

Even as she wrote *The Fountainhead* Rand was experimenting with new ideas and new techniques for later use. Among other things, she began to develop a fascination for the idea of the scientist or engineer as hero. In Steve Ingalls she presents us with a new type. She did one more sketch before tackling her greatest scientist-hero, John Galt. This was Unity 5-3000, the hero of *Anthem*.

The novelette *Anthem* was produced during another interruption of Rand's work on *The Fountainhead*. This short but powerful story provides a further premonition of *Atlas Shrugged*, particularly in stylistic matters. The narrative makes scarcely a pretense of 'romantic realism'; the style is that of fantasy, sometimes more like poem than prose, quite unique among Rand's works. The stylistic influence of Nietzsche is evident, particularly in the eleventh chapter, which is strikingly similar to the opening of *Thus Spoke Zarathustra*. The actual events of the story range from improbable to impossible; it is the ideas that count.

Rand adopts a literary technique popular in the eighteenth and nineteenth centuries, the diary-narrative. The story supposedly is an account written by the hero. The text thus consists solely of a sequence of flashbacks; each chapter jumps ahead in the story, maintaining a high level of suspense until the narrative explains what led up to the new situation. Though old-fashioned, this technique can be highly effective and it is still used (for instance, in Kubrick's *2001: A Space Odyssey*).

The story employs a classically Randian gimmick: In a collectivist, totalitarian world of the future, the very word 'I' has been eliminated from the language. The conflict between individualism and collectivism is thereby reduced to its ultimate fundamentals.

Rand uses this story to illuminate an issue also basic to *The Fountainhead*: the individual as the source of human knowledge and progress. *Anthem*, in contrast to other collectivist dystopias, forecasts no universal electronic surveillance networks, no manipulative biotechnologies, no domed cities or spaceships. Instead, we are shown a collectivist government that has just accomplished, with no small difficulty, the transition from torches to candles. Rand drives home the point by making her hero a self-made scientist, who rediscovers electricity and uses it to make light. The symbolism is effective.

Indeed, Rand may have intended *Anthem* as a response to the influential Russian dystopia *We*, written by Yevgeny Zamiatin in 1920–1921.[6] Like *We*, *Anthem* uses the device of a naive narrator in a world in which names have been replaced by numbers. But here the similarity ends. Zamiatin's hero, like those of *Nineteen Eighty-Four* and *Brave New World*, revolts against an allegedly scientific and logical society in the name of love, poetry, and emotion. D-503, a scientist of the One State, is led into rebellion under the sexual domination of a female mystic. His evident masochism makes his final submission to authority plausible.

Rand, on the other hand, champions reason and science as the enemies of totalitarianism. Her hero, assigned as a street-sweeper, makes himself into a scientist. He is a leader, not a follower, in his rebellion, and his love interest is an adoring and submissive young girl.

The story begins with a superb hook ("It is a sin to write this.") and never drags for an instant. Its inspirational and often poetic narrative is interspersed with just the right amount of Rand's distinctive humor (as for instance the heroine's behavior on her first encounter with a mirror).

In *Anthem*, Rand's concept of the impotence of evil is enhanced and expanded. The men of evil now are seen as almost comically helpless and incompetent, fleeing like roaches from the light created by the book's hero. Like John Galt, *Anthem*'s hero is a scientist and inventor who develops a new source of energy. And the climax, in which he establishes a remote mountain refuge of reason, looks ahead to Galt's Gulch.

'THE SIMPLEST THING IN THE WORLD'

Also written during Rand's transition period was the short story, 'The Simplest Thing in the World'. The hero of this little piece is a talented—and therefore starving—writer. Winning a struggle with his artistic integrity, he resolves to write a piece of hackneyed formula fiction, just to bring in some money. Rand takes this classic cliché and gives it a twist. Her hero sets out to do a potboiler—and finds he can't do it. Not because of his scruples, but simply because every conventional, boring plot idea suddenly takes an ingenious twist.

Rand depicts with a sure hand the petty humiliations of an impecunious man during the Depression, which were so familiar to her. But ultimately the story is frustrating to the reader who would like to hear the full tale of the virtuous blackmailer and the other characters that Rand casually tosses off.

5 | FULL INTEGRATION

With the publication of *Atlas Shrugged* in 1957 Rand reached the destination of her intellectual journey—the Taggart Terminal. She had purged the last vestiges of Nietzsche's errors from her thinking, and completely integrated her ideas into her own philosophical system, Objectivism. The great question of her life, the dilemma of the rational person in an irrational society, at last was solved to her satisfaction. The concept of the "sanction of the victim" provided her answer—and provided also the key plot device, the strike of the men of the mind, for her greatest novel.

Atlas Shrugged, from a purely stylistic or literary point of view, is inferior to *The Fountainhead*. But as an intellectual achievement, it is far superior. A complete, radically new philosophy is expounded, and with astonishing clarity. The practical implications of philosophical ideas are illustrated on every level, from metaphysics to epistemology to ethics to politics to economics to esthetics. The novel's plot is a miracle of organization. And with all this, the book is a thrilling page-turner.

A DEPARTURE IN STYLE

Rand described her fiction style as 'Romantic Realism'. She regarded herself as a Romantic in that her fiction dealt with ideal people and their pursuit of important values; and a Realist in that the settings of her stories and the issues they dealt with were those of real life rather than fantasy. This description is quite appropriate to most of her work. However, *Atlas Shrugged* marks somewhat of a departure. Stylistically, it represents a considerable change from *We the Living* and *The Fountainhead*. Building on the techniques with which she had experimented in *Anthem*, Rand made *Atlas Shrugged* a more abstract, conceptual, and symbolic work than her earlier novels; it might best be described as a work of Romantic Surrealism. The cover painting by George Salter accurately conveys the mood and style of the novel.

Atlas Shrugged takes place in the United States, and cities such as New York and Philadelphia are recognizable. But Rand goes to considerable pains to create an ambiance that is far from realistic. The United States of the novel has no President, but a "Head of State"; no Congress, but a "National Legislature". Most of the world is Communist, but this word does not appear in the book at all; instead, Communist countries are referred to as "People's States". The story takes place in no particular time, and in 'realistic' terms is a tissue of anachronisms. The American economy seems, structurally, to be in the late nineteenth century, with large industrial concerns being sole proprietorships run by their founders. The general tone is however that of the 1930s, a depression with the streets full of panhandlers. The technological level, and the social customs, are those of the 1950s. And the political environment, especially the level of regulation and the total corruption, seems to anticipate the 1970s. We are simultaneously in a future in which most of the world has gone Communist, and the past in which England had the world's greatest navy.

With a subtle choice in literary technique Rand adds to the effective mystery of the story. In *The Fountainhead* Rand adopts the universal viewpoint; we see inside the head of almost every significant character and many very minor ones. (The only important exception is Henry Cameron.) In *Atlas Shrugged* Rand uses what might be called a 'half-universal' viewpoint. We are told the thoughts of nearly every significant character, hero or villain—except the strikers.

In further contrast to Rand's other works, *Atlas Shrugged* is permeated with symbols—from Atlantis to Wyatt's Torch, from

Galt's motor, which draws on the power of the lightning, to Nat Taggart's statue. The symbolic theme of the stopping motor provides a powerful motif throughout the book. And of course there is the famous dollar sign.

JUDAIC SYMBOLISM

One of the paradoxes in Rand's style is her combination of extremely serious philosophical themes and a sense of humor that occasionally verges on the literary equivalent of the practical joke. In *Atlas Shrugged* one of her puckish tricks involves the sly use of Jewish symbolism and myth. For instance, considerable emphasis is laid on Rearden's gift to Dagny of a ruby necklace. It is hard to escape the allusion to the famous biblical quotation:

> Who can find a virtuous woman? for her price is far above rubies. [Proverbs 31:10]

But more interesting is her use of a Talmudic doctrine to provide the basic device of the book: The doctrine of the 36 Just Men. The idea of the 36 Just Men derives from the story, in Genesis, of the destruction of Sodom and Gomorrah. Lot, who resided in the former city, was warned by God to leave, as the place was condemned to destruction because of the evil of its inhabitants. Lot attempted to avert the catastrophe, promising to find other good men in the place; when he failed, he and his family left and the cities were destroyed.

It is interesting to note that—contrary to the popular misconception—the great sin of the Sodomites was not sexual perversion but collectivism. According to the Talmudic account, Sodom's egalitarian government institutionalized envy, even forbidding private charity because some recipients might get more than others. The judicial system was perverted into an instrument for expropriating the wealthy and successful. The ultimate crime for which the Sodomites were destroyed was placing envy and equality above benevolence and justice.

From the biblical account of Sodom and Gomorrah, Jewish scholars evolved the idea that God would destroy the earth if ever it lacked some minimum number of good people. The exact number needed to avert His wrath was hotly debated, and finally settled, for numerological reasons, as 36.

In *Atlas Shrugged*, Rand (who was Jewish by background, though not religious) takes as her theme the destruction of civilization when its 'just men' are withdrawn. The analogy with the 36 Just Men is striking, particularly when one notes that exactly 36 strikers are specifically identified in Galt's Gulch.[1] An incident near the end of the story convinces me that the symbolism is intentional.

As Dagny, Galt, and the other strikers are returning to the valley after rescuing Galt, they pass over New York City. (This in itself is suggestive of some special significance, since New York is nowhere near the great circle route between New Hampshire and Colorado.) As they fly over, the lights of New York go out. Dagny gasps, and Galt orders, "Don't look down!"

What?!

Can this be the same John Galt who said, "Nobody stays in this valley by faking reality in any manner whatsoever."? The incident is totally out of character. And that's Rand's little joke; Galt is saving Dagny from being turned into a pillar of salt.

PLOT, PLOT, AND PLOT

The plot of *Atlas Shrugged* is marvelously constructed, an intricate machine that meshes smoothly with the novel's philosophical themes.

There are, it must be conceded, some notable flaws. For instance, during his affair with Dagny, why does Francisco not tell her about his college friends—Galt and Danneskjold? Obviously this would make hash of the mystery element of the plot, so Rand simply makes Francisco behave out of character. Later she is forced to make Hugh Akston lie to Dagny for the same reason.[2]

A more serious problem is Galt's refusal to let Rearden learn that Dagny is alive, after her crash in the valley. As Nathaniel Branden has pointed out, this gratuitous cruelty does not reflect well on Galt—nor on Dagny.[3] Apparently Rand regarded this incident as essential to the plot; Rearden's loyalty to values, as demonstrated by his continued search for Dagny, is a major factor in her motive for leaving the valley. But surely the dilemma could have been dealt with otherwise.

These are minor problems. Overall, the plot of *Atlas Shrugged* is one of the greatest accomplishments of world literature. Not only is it a masterpiece of logic in itself, but it integrates perfectly the needs of the story with Rand's exposition of a series of philosophical principles. And, with an absolutely insolent arrogance, as if to show off, Rand neatly organizes this extraordinarily complex book into three tidy, cleanly structured sections of ten chapters each.

To analyze the plot of *Atlas Shrugged* thoroughly would require far too much space. But we may consider the main strands.

The primary sequence is the story of how Dagny and Rearden discover the secret of the strike and are led to join it. On the political level, this is integrated with the account of the final destruction of statist society. On the personal level, it is integrated with Dagny's romantic involvement with Francisco, Rearden, and finally Galt. These three strands are braided into the primary plot-line of the novel.

Half-a-dozen subplots are woven into the structure. One is Francisco D'Anconia's Monte-Cristo-like crusade of destruction. Two follow the fates of minor heroes, Eddie Willers and Cherryl Brooks. Three more describe the degradation and destruction of the villains James Taggart, Lillian Rearden, and Robert Stadler. Is this pleasing symmetry intentional? Quite possibly.

THE TECHNIQUE OF PHILOSOPHICAL INTEGRATION

The unifying principle of *Atlas Shrugged* is the connection between philosophical ideas and their consequences. It is worth examining one passage in detail to study Rand's technique. The primary incident in the chapter, 'The Moratorium on Brains', is the catastrophe at the Taggart Tunnel in which an entire passenger train is annihilated. At least one critic has cited this passage as evidence that Rand took a malicious, sadistic pleasure in killing (fictional) people. What is really involved here?

Rand makes the tunnel accident play an important role in the novel's plot mechanics. It brings Dagny back from her self-imposed exile so that she can receive Quentin Daniels' letter. It interrupts Francisco's explanation of the strike at a crucial point, and sets up the confrontation between Francisco and Hank Rearden in Dagny's apartment. The disaster also necessitates the journey that will put her on a frozen train and propel her into her meeting with John Galt.

The sequence also plays an important part in a more subtle aspect of the plot, by beginning the process of final preparation for Dagny to be confronted with the secret of the strike. The first step is Directive 10-289. Dagny's instinctive rejection of this irrational horror results in her resignation from Taggart Transcontinental. But this, to Rand, could not be a satisfactory resolution; Dagny must reach this stage of emotional revulsion, but she could not be Rand's heroine if she made her decision on the basis of emotion. What has been accomplished however is that Dagny (and the reader) have been presented with the solution to the novel's dilemma—the strike.

Dagny's resignation is followed by a month of meditation in the woods, in which for the first time her basic dilemma is made explicit. Then the pressure is turned up. Francisco appears to present her with the key concept of the sanction of the victim. It is at this point that the tunnel catastrophe intervenes. Francisco fails to recruit Dagny—because Dagny, having quit due to emotional revulsion, returns due to emotional revulsion.

It is important to understand that Dagny's emotional reaction to the disaster plays a critical role. She is not merely annoyed by a sublime piece of incompetence. She is not just outraged by the destruction of an important item of her railroad's property. She is horrified by the human destruction, the loss of life. Rand is building up here to a major, dual climax in the novel's plot: Dagny's discovery of the secret of the strike, and her meeting with John Galt. The tunnel catastrophe plays a key role in building the tension that will be (partially and temporarily) resolved in Galt's Gulch.

During this chapter Dagny is put under increasing emotional stress, until she nears the breaking point. Directive 10-289 drives her from her job in disgust—and separates her from Rearden (on whom it also puts pressure). Her month in the woods wrestling with an insoluble problem focusses her emotional state. Then there is the astounding revelation that Francisco is in fact faithful to her—a scene interrupted by the report of the tunnel catastrophe. The sequence continues with the confrontation between Rearden and Francisco, which raises the tension of Dagny's sexual relationship with Rearden to a maximum. We can begin to see how masterfully Rand pulls these two strands of the plot together in preparation for Dagny's encounter with Galt.

But the Taggart Tunnel catastrophe is not merely an incident in the plot; it also functions as a demonstration of an important principle: the relationship between political oppression and the breakdown of social responsibility—and the consequent destruction of social function. Rand in this chapter provides us with a vivid picture of the way even everyday activities disintegrate when the men of ability and rationality are driven underground. This is the function of the scene on the book's philosophical or intellectual level.

Rand begins preparation for this scene early and carefully ties it into the other events of the plot. Early in the story we learn of the bad condition of the Taggart track near Winston, Colorado. Accidents happen on this stretch of the road. The need to repair it is casually mentioned. But it is merely a nuisance, a potential problem.

With Dagny's resignation, Rand begins her demonstration. First, the repairs at Winston are cancelled; the rail instead is used on the Florida line, which is more frequently travelled by politicians. This decision is allowed to stand—because Dagny is gone. Then the spare diesel at the Taggart Tunnel is withdrawn, again to please a politician. Eddie Willers attempts to stop it, but with Dagny gone he is helpless.

The process by which the accident happens is, to anyone acquainted with industrial safety principles, entirely realistic. It is exactly the sort of sequence which creates real-life disasters such as the Bhopal and Chernobyl accidents.

The petty politician Kip Chalmers, inconvenienced by a derailment near Winston, insists on immediate continuation of his journey—through the tunnel—though no diesel engines are available. The men of intelligence and integrity, who could prevent the ensuing catastrophe, are gone because of Directive 10-289, just as Dagny is. The best of those who remain are, like Eddie, of insufficient rank to intervene successfully. One by one, the safeguards set by rational men are violated by political appointees, driven by their fear of political reprisals.

It would take only one man to prevent the tragedy—but that

one man is not present any more. The Superintendent of the Division has been replaced by an incompetent. Higher management, with Dagny gone, evades all responsibility. The one man who fights the disaster, Bill Brent, lacks authority. The physical order is signed by a boy who lacks knowledge.

So the inexorable march to disaster continues. The dispatcher knows he is sending men to their deaths. But he no longer cares; his beloved brother committed suicide, his career ruined by Directive 10-289. It appears that disaster may be averted when the chosen engineer walks out rather than take a coal-burner into the Tunnel—but a replacement is found, an alcoholic who kept his job by political pull and union corruption. The conductor, who might have warned the passengers, has become embittered and cynical; he limits his action to saving himself. Even the switchman might have averted the wreck at the last minute. But in the new environment of the railroad, he fears for his family if he disobeys orders, even to save lives.

So the Comet proceeds into the tunnel. And with magnificent irony Kip Chalmers, having succeeded in scaring the Taggart employees into sending him to his death, proudly proclaims, "See? *Fear* is the only effective way to deal with people!"

RAND'S HEROES: THE ROOTS

By her own account, in *Atlas Shrugged* Rand finally succeeded in portraying her ideal man, John Galt. And indeed, she has met the challenge of showing completely moral persons in a way that she did not achieve in *The Fountainhead*. Dominique and Wynand are, as we have seen, contaminated by Nietzschean morality and the corresponding despair. Roark is morally perfect, but he is not a full ideal because he is naive. He is good without knowing fully why he is good. John Galt, however, has moral stature and philosophical knowledge.

Atlas Shrugged has a complex plot involving a number of major and minor heroic characters. Rand takes as her primary heroes the giants of intellect and productivity, particularly business entrepreneurs. The basic fabric of these characters derives from the hero of one of her favorite books, Merwin and Webster's *Calumet K*. Charlie Bannon, an engineer and construction supervisor, a natural leader and compulsive worker who solves problems with effortless ingenuity, is described as skeletally thin. Appropriately, Rand fleshes out this skeleton with full personalities to create her business heroes.

The modern reader may not realize how radical it was, in 1957, to make a businessman a hero. It should be kept in mind that Rand wrote this book in an environment in which 'entrepreneur' was almost a dirty word. It is interesting to note, however, that there was one other significant writer of the period who defended businessmen, and who may have influenced Rand: Cameron Hawley.

In Hawley's second novel, *Cash McCall* (1955), the theme is ethical conflicts in business, and the author comes down squarely for the position that commerce is an honorable activity. McCall is what would now be called a 'corporate raider', and Hawley skillfully depicts his economic value and productiveness.

Even more interesting for our discussion is the theme of Hawley's first novel, *Executive Suite* (1952). This is the story of a struggle for control of a major company after its CEO, Avery Bullard, suddenly dies. Here is the scene in which the hero, looking out over the company town, decides it is his responsibility to take over the leaderless corporation:

> They were his . . . all of them . . . the uncounted thousands, born and unborn. If he failed them there would be hunger under those roofs . . . there had been hunger before when the man at the top of the Tower had failed them. Then there would be no food . . . and the belongings of the dispossessed would stand in the streets . . . and a man in a black coat would come to take the children to the orphans' home . . .
>
> . . . Did the people under those roofs know what Avery Bullard had done for them? Did they realize that if it had not been for Avery Bullard there would be no Tredway Corporation . . . that the Pike Street plant would never have been built . . . that the Water Street factory would have rotted and rusted away like the steel mill and the tannery and the wagon works . . . that there would be no Tredway jobs, no Tredway paychecks?
>
> No, they did not know . . . or, if they did, they would not acknowledge their belief . . . or, if they believed, they were not willing to pay the price of gratitude. Had any man ever thanked Avery Bullard for what he had done? No. He had died in the loneliness of the unthanked.
>
> Don Walling accepted his fate. He would expect no thanks . . . he would live in loneliness . . . but the Tredway Corporation would go on. There would be jobs and pay checks. There would be no hunger. The belongings

of the dispossessed would not stand in the streets. No children would be sent to the orphans' home.[4]

Though the motives of Hawley's character are hardly those of an Objectivist, the theme of the entrepreneurial businessman as an unappreciated hero who gives society far more than can ever be repaid clearly prefigures Rand's use of the same theme. There is no external evidence to support it, but she may well have been influenced by Hawley's heroes. (She would certainly, however, have been disgusted by *The Lincoln Lords* [1960], which idealizes a man who bears no small resemblance to Peter Keating.)

Into the gray-suited bodies of her business executive heroes Rand poured the souls of her childhood idols from the melodramas she devoured as a girl. There resulted those extraordinary characters who have inspired so many of her young readers—especially the central heroes of *Atlas Shrugged*, Dagny Taggart and the three men who become her lovers: Francisco D'Anconia, Hank Rearden, and John Galt.

DAGNY TAGGART AND THE RANDIAN WOMAN

In Dagny Taggart Rand creates her ideal woman. Her earlier female protagonists are mostly Nietzschean and, as such, tragic figures. Dominique Francon, it is true, renounces her allegiance to Nietzsche, but this decision does not come until nearly the end of *The Fountainhead*, so that we can only project what her life and personality will be like as an Objectivist. Gaia, the teenaged heroine of *Anthem*, is not a well-developed character. It is only with the appearance of Dagny that we can see how Rand visualizes the 'ideal' woman.

Dagny, like the other heroes of *Atlas Shrugged*, is an incarnation of the virtue of competence. In her mid-thirties she is the de facto CEO of the country's largest railroad. Intelligent, decisive, self-confident, she embodies the prime characteristic of the natural leader: she is the person who knows what to do.

As one might expect from Rand's literary technique, Dagny's characterization is rooted in a seeming paradox. On the one hand, she appears neuter, if not masculine, in her aggressiveness and career dedication. Lillian Rearden describes her as "an adding machine in tailored suits". When Cherryl Taggart claims her place as the woman of the Taggart family, Dagny responds, "That's quite all right. I'm the man."

On the other hand, Dagny is an intensely feminine woman. (She is, in fact, the kind of woman who wears a dress and stockings to explore an abandoned factory!) She is attracted to strong, dominant men, and desires to play an explicitly submissive role in her sexual relationships.

The key to the seeming contradiction is that Dagny has repressed her sexuality in the hostile society in which she exists. Dagny's air of coldness and unemotional, pseudo-masculine behavior are a consequence of her immersion in a society which contains nobody to whom she can respond naturally. This is hinted at in Rand's depiction of the Rearden anniversary party, at which Dagny is described as presenting a challenge which nobody can perceive. There is a vivid contrast between Dagny's unexpressed personality in the statist world and her temperament in Galt's Gulch, where she happily becomes—a housewife! That this was Rand's conscious intention is shown by her notes for *Atlas Shrugged*:

> Dagny, who is considered so hard, cold, heartless, and domineering, is actually the most emotional, passionate, tender, and gay-hearted person of all—but only Galt can bring it out. Her other aspect is what the world forces on her or deserves from her.[5]

Rand herself was profoundly ambivalent on the issue of feminism. She was a strong advocate of careers for women, of course, and said (in her *Playboy* interview), "There is no particular work which is specifically feminine." She endorsed (with some political reservations) Betty Friedan's *The Feminine Mystique*. She was contemptuous of 'housewives' in general. On the abortion issue, Rand took a vigorously 'pro-choice' position.

Yet Rand could scarcely be classified as a feminist. Though most of her heroines lack interest in marriage and family life, there are exceptions. Gaia, in *Anthem*, shows no ambition beyond following her man, and is pregnant at the end of the novel. Rand sympathetically portrays the anonymous young woman who chooses motherhood as a 'profession' in Galt's Gulch, as well as Mrs. William Hastings, who appears to be a 'mere' housewife.

Rand's notorious statement that a woman ought not to aspire to be President of the United States hardly sounds like feminism. And, in response to a question about her position (at her 1981 Ford Hall Forum appearance) she said, "I'm a male chauvinist."

Rand could hardly have meant by this—in a literal dictionary sense—that she exhibited "unreasoning devotion" to the male sex and contempt for the female sex. She did not say that men in general are superior to women. What, then, did she mean? Consider this:

> Hero-worship is a demanding virtue: a woman has to be worthy of it and of the hero she worships. Intellectually and morally, i.e., as a human being, she has to be his equal; then the object of her worship is specifically his masculinity, not any human virtue she might lack.[6]

Later in the same essay, Rand says, "[the feminine woman's] worship is an abstract emotion for the metaphysical concept of masculinity as such". It appears that Rand would attach a special, exceptional value to 'masculinity' as 'the fact of being a man', and that she was a 'male chauvinist' in this sense. Rand is explicit that the feminine woman's desire to look up to man "does not mean dependence, obedience or anything implying inferiority".

When we examine Rand's fictional heroines, we find that they certainly exhibit this intense admiration for the masculinity of their lovers. But, despite Rand's stated opinions, her fiction suggests that she regarded men as being inherently superior to women. Gaia, for instance, is far from being an intellectual equal of her mate. For that matter, Dominique does not seem to be quite a match for Howard Roark in ability, nor Dagny for John Galt.

All Rand's heroines are explicitly submissive in a sexual sense. Indeed, it is hard to avoid the suggestion of a certain degree of masochism in the physically vigorous couplings of Dagny and Rearden, in Faulkner's burning Karen Andre with hot platinum, and of course in Dominique's first sexual encounter with Roark.

Rand herself married a man who was far from being a John Galt in intellectual stature. Frank O'Connor, protective, nurturing, and pliable, gave her the emotional support of a husband without the inconvenient demands. She could pursue her career as she wished, and he accommodated her. Like Dagny, she was the man in her family.

But she really didn't want to be a man. Her struggle over the decades compelled her to become mannish in many ways; a 'womanly' woman could never have waged the war Rand fought. Yet through it all she battled to remain a woman. The desire to reclaim and assert her femininity, contends Barbara Branden, impelled her into the affair with Nathaniel Branden.[7]

One can find a psychological explanation for Rand's portrayal of the sexes in her personal conflict. As a woman she longed for a mate who could match or even surpass her ability, a hero who would fill her need for romance and passion, a man who would dominate her sexually. Yet hero-worship has its obligations as well as its privileges; a marriage with a real-life John Galt, even if she could have found one, would have imposed demands she could never have accepted. Nothing could be allowed to interfere with her intellectual growth or achievements. Devastating as this paradox was to her personal happiness, its tension contributed to her art, in which she portrayed a series of fascinating man-woman relationships.

From a more abstract point of view, Rand's vision of men and women reflects her uncritical acceptance of the twentieth-century cliché that human behavior has no genetic component. Accepting that humans are born *"tabula rasa"*—blank slates—she could not develop a theory of sexuality that accounted for the inherent differences between the sexes in a coherent manner. As we will see, this contradiction also had its effect on the Objectivist ethics.

Rand may not have understood what made the male sex an ideal for her, but she knew what she liked, and the heroes of *Atlas Shrugged* demonstrate her vision of man at his best.

Francisco D'Anconia

Francisco Domingo Carlos Andres Sebastian D'Anconia is the favorite character of many readers of *Atlas Shrugged*. Like Dagny, he embodies a paradox: He is at once a man of extraordinary *joie de vivre*, gay, light-hearted, sophisticated; and a man of tragedy, frozen, unemotional, implacable.

The light side of Francisco embodies the sense of life that Rand aspired to, the unobstructed, effortless achievement of joy in a totally benevolent universe. As the young boy who can do anything, and do it superbly, who fears nothing and hates nobody, he presents an extraordinarily attractive figure.

The other side of the coin is the tortured but self-controlled man who allows no feeling or suffering to affect him, much less deflect him. His relentless pursuit of his terrible purpose invokes our awe and admiration.

We love Francisco precisely because of the union of these aspects of his personality. It was a stroke of artistic genius to create a character paradoxically embodying these disparate traits, and it is a tribute to Rand's literary skill that she could integrate them into a convincing personality.

Hank Rearden

Hank Rearden is older than the other major heroes of *Atlas Shrugged*. (He is 45 as the novel opens.) He also presents a different sort of inner conflict. Unlike Dagny, he feels a fundamental sense of guilt, which has been carefully nurtured over the years by his wife, the despicable Lillian. He has responded by emotional withdrawal.

It is critical to emphasize that Rand does not present Rearden's obsessive fixation with his business as an ideal. On the contrary, his struggle with emotional repression is a key thread of the plot.

We see Rearden, when he is first introduced, as a man who is interested in nothing but steel. He literally falls asleep when forced to deal with any other topic. The only hint that he is anything beyond a stereotypical workaholic is a jade vase in his office.

But this is not the real Rearden. As his affair with Dagny flowers, he expands as a person. Without losing his passionate commitment to his career, he begins to develop the full personality that he had so long repressed. He takes an interest in ideas, begins to express his love of beauty, becomes more relaxed and gay. As this process unfolds, his emotions open up. He finds himself able to love Dagny. He also responds more effectively to his co-workers; his relationship with his secretary, Gwen Ives, visibly expands and becomes more personal as his affair with Dagny progresses. And he is able to de-repress his resentment of, and contempt for, his worthless family.

Much of the novel is devoted to showing Rearden's gradual emotional blossoming, as he responds to Dagny and to Francisco D'Anconia. This is a vital factor in the plot; before he can join the strikers, he must not only deal with his unearned guilt, but he must establish new, interpersonal values so that his mills are not the be-all of his life—otherwise he could not abandon them.

WHO *IS* JOHN GALT?

To depict an ideal man in a work of literature is a difficult assignment for any author. Few have attempted it; none have attempted such an ambitious ideal as does Rand.

John Galt, by the nature of the novel's plot, carries a heavy burden to start with. As the leader of the strikers, and the core of the novel's mystery element, he does not even appear on stage (except in disguise) until the last third of the book. We see him for two chapters; then he again disappears until the book's climax. Galt receives so little exposure to the reader that only Rand's superb technique can make him real at all.

Unfortunately, it is not quite sufficient to fully expand his character. John Galt, like Howard Roark, is too perfect to sustain a convincing internal conflict. Indeed, Galt was explicitly intended to represent man-become-god, and Rand deliberately avoided any details of characterization that might have made him seem more 'human' in the usual, self-deprecatory sense of the word. John Galt is Rand's ultimate answer to Nietzsche; he is an assertion that we need not evolve any 'superman', that man can become godlike himself if he so chooses.

But of course, the Randian paradox appears as always. John Galt, the ideal man, the pinnacle of the human species, is condemned to work underground, as a greasy laborer in the Taggart tunnels. This idea, that in a corrupt society the best men will be found at the bottom, plays a part in all of Rand's novels. Kira encounters Leo in a red-light district. In *The Fountainhead* Dominique discovers Howard Roark working, like a slave or a convict, in a quarry. The hero of *Anthem* is assigned as a street-sweeper and does his illicit scientific work in an abandoned subway tunnel—underground.

(An interesting inversion takes place in the strikers' valley. Galt, the lowly trackworker, becomes the revered leader of society. And Dagny, the wealthy executive, finds herself penniless and must find work as a maid.)

Galt was not merely Rand's ideal man; he was the projection of Rand herself. He verges on pure intellect; he is a philosopher and teacher; he is the leader of an intellectual movement; and he is, through most of his life, frustrated by the inability to find a partner worthy of him.

If John Galt sometimes seems more a symbol than a person, it reflects Rand's difficulty in visualizing her ideal man. When she tried, she ran up against the contradiction implicit in her *tabula rasa* model of humanity: to be an ideal man, John Galt would have to be inherently different from a woman. He would have to be distinctively male, not just a pure intellect happening to inhabit a male body. Just as Rand could not make herself fully female, so she could not make her ideal hero fully male. Her concept of humanity, for all its novel and perceptive insights, was incomplete.

BIT-PART HEROES

The story includes a number of heroes who spend but little time on stage: Lawrence Hammond, Roger Marsh, Midas Mulligan, Kay Ludlow, and many others. Rand herself makes a cameo appearance as the writer/fishwife in the valley, who nurses a hopeless passion for Galt.

Some of these characters are relegated to simple supporting roles. Others, such as Dr. Hendricks and Richard Halley, function as vehicles for short speeches on specialized topics. Only a few play a significant part in the plot. Ragnar Danneskjold, the philosopher-turned-pirate, is of course the most prominent of these. Hugh Akston, Dan Conway, and Ellis Wyatt also play key roles.

It is a tribute to Rand's literary talent that she makes most of these minor characters real and distinct personalities, though none receives more than a few paragraphs of text.

THE VILLAINS

Rand also creates an incredible rogues' gallery of villains, and provides them with some beautifully appropriate names: Wesley

Mouch, Tinky Holloway, and Cuffy Meigs are classics. Floyd Ferris has just the right ring for the handsome, slick, and vicious scientist-bureaucrat. Robert Stadler's name gives a hint of the statist views which make him a villain. Perhaps best suited of all is that undistinguished politician Mr. Thompson, an old-fashioned gangster very similar in style to the weapon suggested by his name.

Though Rand has been criticized for creating two-dimensional villains, the fact is that she devotes considerable effort to digging into the psychology of evil. Three villains are analyzed in considerable depth: James Taggart, Lillian Rearden, and Robert Stadler.

Jim Taggart is visualized by most readers as short, fat, and ugly; some critics have even attacked Rand for making all her villains physically unprepossessing. This is a tribute to her skill; the actual description of Jim Taggart in the book is as tall, slim, and aristocratic in appearance. It is the reader who unconsciously visualizes him as ugly, giving him a physical appearance to fit his character.

For ugly he is—psychologically. A man of mediocre talent, he inherits control of Taggart Transcontinental. At the opening of the story, he is 39 and a neurotic whose response to the problems of the railroad he nominally heads is, "Don't bother me, don't bother me, don't bother me." Gradually we watch his psychological disintegration, until he ends up as a catatonic. He is unable to face the fact that he is "a killer—for the sake of killing", and psychosis is ultimately his only escape.

Lillian Rearden is a marvelous portrayal. She is a fitting foil for Dagny: intelligent, capable of shrewd psychological insight, and completely dedicated to relentless pursuit of a single goal. Her campaign to destroy Hank Rearden is masterfully conceived and flawlessly executed. It is only his extraordinary inner strength, and some timely help from Dagny and Francisco, that saves him.

In the story of Dr. Robert Stadler, Rand achieves a Trollopian depiction of temptation and the consequences of surrender to it. When we first see Stadler, he is a great mind, a brilliant scientist, who has compromised with statism to get the money to continue his research. This initial sin inexorably presents him with a series of moral dilemmas, and each failure to turn back leads him deeper into the morass.

In his first crisis, the State Science Institute issues an attack on Rearden Metal. Though Stadler knows it is false, he dares not contradict it, for fear that the Institute's funding might be reduced. Later Floyd Ferris attacks science and reason explicitly, and even uses Stadler's name in doing so. This time Stadler protests—but not publicly. Ferris goes on to create Project X, using Stadler's discoveries to forge a weapon of terror. And now, under Directive 10-289, the consequences of rebellion are more serious; Stadler faces not mere embarrassment but the threat of starvation. Under compulsion, he publicly praises his tormentors and commends them for their perversion of the knowledge he had created. By the novel's end Stadler has surrendered utterly to corruption, and his last act in life is an undignified scuffle with a drunken criminal for possession of the murderous weapon he had once scorned.

Most of Rand's villains fill bit parts. The mystic Ivy Starnes, the whining Lee Hunsaker, the pretentious Gilbert Keith-Worthing, and many others are portrayed with a few deft strokes and used as needed. Each, however, is used to make a unique point.

Rand is careful, despite her 'black and white' moral code, to avoid any hint of moral determinism. One villain, the "Wet Nurse", demonstrates that it is possible to turn away from evil. Another, the labor racketeer Fred Kinnan, shows a certain blunt honesty that makes him more sympathetic than his colleagues.

THE SECONDARY HEROES

Perhaps the most neglected characters in discussion of *Atlas Shrugged* are what one might call the 'lesser heroes'—people who are morally good, but lack the immense ability of Dagny and the other strikers. Rand treats sympathetically such tiny roles as the police chief of Durrance (who helps Dagny locate the Starnes heirs) and Mrs. William Hastings. Another such character, the hobo Jeff Allen, supplies a key piece of information in the main mystery of the plot. Three of these characters, however, receive considerable attention: Tony (the "Wet Nurse"), Cherryl Brooks, and Eddie Willers.

Tony, the young, amoral bureaucrat who is sent to supervise Rearden's production under the "Fair Share Law", represents the human potential for moral redemption. At his first appearance, he is a total cynic. The very concept of morality has been educated out of him, so that he finds Rearden's integrity disturbing and incomprehensible. Gradually, in the productive environment of the Rearden mills, he develops a desire for an ideal to believe in. Tony begins to feel admiration and sympathy for Rearden. He offers assistance in bribing the bureaucracy to obtain higher quotas, which Rearden of course rejects. Later, when Rearden defies the State Science Institute's order for Rearden Metal, Tony is concerned for Rearden's safety and chides him for taking such a risk. His commitment to Rearden becomes progressively stronger: he cheers Rearden's triumph at his trial; he fails to report Rearden's violations of regulations, and later volunteers to actively conceal them; he asks Rearden to let him quit the bureaucracy and work for the mill, even if only in a menial job. In the end he has accepted Rearden's ideals and fights to defend them; Tony's murder is the final straw before Rearden joins the strike.

Cherryl Brooks is the most tragic character of *Atlas Shrugged*. She is a slum girl determined to rise. (Had the book been written ten years later, Rand might well have made Cherryl a Black.) She is not brilliant, not an intellectual, has no career ambitions. But she is fiercely honest, idealistic, and courageous. Finding herself married far 'above her station' to James Taggart, she applies her limited ability to the task she considers appropriate to her: becoming a high-society 'lady'. Zealously she studies etiquette, culture, and style to become the kind of wife Taggart, in her vision of him, deserves. And she succeeds; the slum girl from the five-and-dime transforms herself into a sophisticated member of the aristocracy of wealth. Again we see a classic Randian cliché-reversal. Taking off from Shaw's *Pygmalion*, Rand invents an Eliza Doolittle who transforms herself into a lady on her own initiative and by her own efforts—against the opposition of her 'benefactor', who wants her to remain a slum girl. But Cherryl's effort to become a worthy consort for her husband goes for nothing; Taggart is not a hero but a rotter; he has married her, not to ennoble her, but to destroy her.

The most important of the lesser heroes is Dagny's assistant, Eddie Willers, the very first character to whom we are introduced as the novel opens. It is easy to underestimate Eddie Willers. Standing beside Dagny Taggart or Hank Rearden he seems ordinary, not very competent, almost a bit wimpish. This, however, is due merely to the contrast with Rand's extraordinary heroes, as the moon seems dim in sunlight. Hank Rearden, who ought to know, says that Eddie has the makings of a good business-man. In fact, he is a highly able executive. Toward the end of the book, he bribes his way onto an Army plane and flies into a city torn apart by civil war. In the space of a few days, singlehanded, he negotiates immunity with three separate warring factions, reorganizes the Taggart terminal, revitalizes its personnel, and gets the trains running again. Some wimp!

All three of these lesser heroes come to bad ends. Tony is mur-dered when he defies his masters and attempts to warn Rearden of the plot against his mills. Cherryl commits suicide when she discovers the horrifying truth about her husband. Eddie strands himself in the desert, sobbing at the foot of a dead locomotive. Why is there no happy ending for these characters?

Mimi Gladstein suggests that Eddie's fate is punishment for his refusal to accompany Dagny to Galt's Gulch.[8] Certainly it is a consequence of that decision, but it is wrong to see it as punish-ment for a moral failing.

In her treatment of the lesser heroes Rand expresses an impor-tant truth. The essence of statism is the destruction of all that is good in the human spirit. The ablest heroes frequently escape, to make new lives for themselves elsewhere. Such people as Rachmaninoff and Sikorsky and Rand escaped from the Bolsheviks. Such people as Einstein and Fermi and von Mises escaped from the Nazis. Rand evokes the tragedy of the ordinary people that perished at Vorkuta or Auschwitz. These were the people who attempted to fight, but lacked the ability to do so effectively—like Tony. Or they were the people who died of sheer despair, facing a horror beyond their conception—like Cherryl. Or, they were those who might have escaped, but could not bring themselves to give up their old life and start over again with no capital but their own minds—like Eddie. Rand had known such people; her own father died under the Soviet regime, unwilling to leave Russia and give up the hope that he might somehow get his business back. She pities them, does not condemn them.

THE BRANDEN CRITIQUE

Since his break with Rand, Nathaniel Branden has raised a number of criticisms of *Atlas Shrugged*. Though the book, as is inevitable for such an ambitious undertaking, falls short of perfection, several of Branden's points of attack are not justified. Yet he is a perceptive critic, and his objections are worth serious consideration.

Branden criticizes as psychologically unrealistic, and indeed downright reprehensible, Francisco D'Anconia's twelve-year, self-imposed celibacy in faithfulness to Dagny. For a man of Francisco's vitality to accept such a trial verges, in Branden's judgment, on self-sacrifice.[9]

Branden makes a good point here, and in a later commentary[10] points out an even stronger example. How about John Galt? His ordeal is nearly as long as Francisco's, after all. And this perfect man, Rand's ideal hero, is, it appears, a virgin at the age of 37 when he finally consummates his love for Dagny in the Taggart tunnels.

This behavior, both Francisco's and Galt's, is in fact absurd—or rather it would be, if *Atlas Shrugged* were a naturalistic or even realistic novel. But if we look at the book as it is—as a work of romantic surrealism which is heavily laden with symbolism—we can see that incidents such as this should be taken as the symbols they are, not as literal prescriptions for human behavior. Francisco and Galt exhibit this uncompromising loyalty to values—'price no object'—to reinforce Rand's ethical point.

Branden makes a more substantive criticism of the scene in which Dagny encounters Jeff Allen on the Taggart Comet. She watches indifferently as the conductor orders him to jump off the train, to certain death. Dagny intervenes only when the tramp, exhibiting a "sense of property", tightens his grip on his belongings. This, to Branden, exhibits a brutal indifference to human life.

Branden errs here by taking the scene completely out of its emotional context in the novel. Suppose we look at it not as an isolated incident but as part of a complex plot, an integral component of the sequence we analyzed above.

Dagny, at this point in the novel, is riding the first Comet to run after the tunnel catastrophe. She had resigned in disgust on the issuance of Directive 10-289; but she was unable to maintain her resolve when the disaster demonstrated the consequences of her absence. She has also just received a series of terrible shocks. She has discovered that Francisco is not, after all, the rotter she thought him, that indeed he still loves her and is worthy of her love. Close on this has followed the devastating encounter between Rearden and Francisco. Then follows the news that Quentin Daniels, the last hope of reconstructing the motor, has quit. Pervading all is her despair—trapped, unable either to quit or to enjoy her work—functioning as a slave, and as a slave-driver— the men she had trusted and respected on the railroad gone—the workers, once her friends, now treating her, deservedly, as an enemy—and above all her loneliness. There is no one on the train she can care for or respect, it seems. Francisco's words ring in her head: "But you would not run trains if they were empty."

It is at this point, and in this mood, that Dagny walks in on the conductor and Jeff Allen in the vestibule of her private car. After what she has been through in the last few days, it is not easy to care about these two strangers. So what if a tramp dies? So what if the whole human race dies? But then a simple gesture reminds her that there are human values in the world. Suddenly the context of her life and her values is regained, and she says, "Wait. Let him be my guest."

In fact this short scene, only a few paragraphs, provides an excellent example of Rand's psychological insight and literary skill. With effortless accuracy she portrays Dagny's moment of despair and rage, and her resilient recovery.

RAND AND REPRESSION

Branden's strongest criticism of *Atlas Shrugged* is that it teaches the reader to repress emotions.[10] While acknowledging that Rand explicitly rejects and condemns repression, and indeed provides many examples of emotional openness, he nonetheless insists that the tone of the book, taken as a whole, encourages repression.

This raises a difficult issue. To what extent can an author be held responsible for the misinterpretation of his work by his readers? For this is misinterpretation. To anyone who was a part of the Objectivist movement of the Sixties, it is obvious that many of Rand's readers felt encouraged to repress emotions under the social pressures applied by some of the movement's cadre. Yet—objectively!—*Atlas Shrugged* contains a powerful attack on repression. Over and over again, Rand emphasizes that life in an irrational society creates the danger of emotional repression. One of the key ideas of the novel is that the able and rational person is capable of emotional freedom only in the context of social relationships with others of his kind.

The entire story of Hank Rearden is a devastating depiction of the dangers of emotional repression. Take as just one instance the scene in which Rearden, walking to Dagny's apartment after a meeting with copper producers, realizes that he has lost his sexual desire for her. At the conference he has learned that new government regulations will devastate the copper industry, and he has failed to find a solution. Worse, he is told that the regulations resulted from a deal involving Francisco D'Anconia. Repressing the pain—his frustration, his feeling of failure, and most especially the apparent betrayal by Francisco—he represses also his ability to respond to Dagny. Rand's depiction of this repression—its causes—its consequences—and its removal—is psychologically completely accurate. This scene is only one of many in which Rand explicitly shows the danger of emotional repression. Please note that Rand does not talk or moralize here about repression; she doesn't even mention the word. She demonstrates by her characters' behavior.

Repeatedly Rand emphasizes this point, using character after character—Ellis Wyatt, Quentin Daniels, and especially Francisco D'Anconia, to demonstrate the contrast between the frozen, embittered, restricted emotional states of heroes trapped in the evil 'outside' world, and the openness and freedom of their behavior in the valley. If anyone still feels that *Atlas Shrugged* promotes emotional repression, let him read the scene in which Dagny encounters Ken Danagger immediately after he has joined the strike.

Now admittedly, much of this goes right over the head of even a very intelligent teenager; but is Rand at fault? We may, if we wish, accept Branden's testimony that Rand herself, and the circle around her, encouraged emotional repression in her students. But, on the evidence, *Atlas Shrugged* does the opposite.

Could the vision of extraordinary emotional control presented by Rand's heroes inspire young people to pay too little attention to their emotions? The danger, alas, seems remote. As Jane Austen's Mr. Bennet sarcastically put it, "You may well warn me against such an error; human nature is so prone to fall into it."

If we are to criticize Rand's influence on young people, I would be inclined to raise a different issue. Rand repeatedly depicts heroes who choose their careers in early childhood and never deviate from their course. Even the brightest of children lack the experience needed to make a rational career choice as teenagers. I suspect that more of Rand's readers have suffered through trying to emulate her heroes by committing themselves to ill-chosen vocations, than through becoming emotionally repressed.

But any such objection to Rand's characterization of her heroes, including mine, is fundamentally unfair. Unquestionably a great part of Ayn Rand's appeal to young people flows from her presentation of heroes they can admire and emulate. The present generation of youth are starved for such heroes, just as were Branden's generation, and mine. Let them get from Rand what they need. Some, no doubt, will fail to understand the full context of her characters and will adopt inappropriate behavior; that danger is inherent in emulation. But better to take that risk than to have no heroes at all.

THE RANDIAN LOVERS

Finally, Branden has made some strong criticisms of Rand's depiction of love and sex, based primarily on analysis of *Atlas Shrugged*.[10] This seems an appropriate place to consider his points.

Unlike many critics, Branden does not see Rand's "male chauvinism" (as she herself called it) and preference for male sexual dominance as "a sexist issue". Taken in the context of the story, he considers these attitudes appropriate for her heroines. For similar reasons, he does not criticize the famous 'rape' scene in *The Fountainhead*.

Branden sees as positive aspects of Rand's love scenes two factors. First, Rand presents admiration as a key ingredient of romantic love. Second, as a corollary, Rand promotes dignity in the treatment of romantic partners.

However, Branden emphatically denies the root concept of Rand's theory of romantic love: that a person is determined by his philosophical premises and that sexual desire and love are responses to those premises.[11] Instead, Branden says, sexual psychology is very complex and there are many factors involved in arousing sexual desire for a certain person.

If Branden intends to say that these other factors *in addition to* basic values determine romantic choice, it is hard to quarrel with his argument—and it is not clear that Rand would. After all, she did not portray Dagny as being sexually attracted to all the strikers equally, though presumably they all share the philosophical values of John Galt. It would seem obvious that there must be something more than philosophical premises determining romantic choices. Perhaps Rand should have added another speech to the novel to explain these factors in more detail? If, however, Branden believes that response to values is not important in romantic choice, one would like to hear him expound his theory more fully before rejecting Rand's.

Branden's major criticism of Rand's attitudes toward love and sex, as exhibited in *Atlas Shrugged*, is "lack of psychological realism". As mentioned before, he cites the celibacy of Francisco and of Galt as totally unrealistic. Branden further suggests that Rearden and Francisco's lack of sexual jealousy and depression when Dagny becomes Galt's lover shows a psychological resiliency which is not just superhuman but inhuman. He also complains that Rand fails to show intimacy and warmth between her lovers. To Branden, this lack of realism amounts to the projection of unattainable ideals which may lead readers (particularly young readers) to dismiss romantic love as being impossible to real people.

If Branden's analysis is taken as a warning to readers not to unthinkingly adopt the behavior of Rand's characters as a literal prescription, one can scarcely fault it. But as a literary critic, Branden, in accusing her of demanding too much of her readers, is himself demanding too much of the author. Though he expresses valid concerns, they are based on an unrealistic idea of what a novelist—even a genius—can accomplish in one book. It is not enough, it seems, to expound a radically new system of philosophy from top to bottom—to delineate dozens of characters and make them real—to build an extraordinarily complex plot—and to tie everything together with scarcely a loose end. No, every idea must be worked out not just in broad strokes, but in detail. Each character must, like an over-ambitious actor pestering the director for more lines, have the chance to display every facet of his personality. The plot must include not just the essential action but enough to make sure that even the most naive reader will not mistake the meaning of events.

It is simply too much. Dr. Branden has expressed the desire to write a novel himself. Would he wish to be held to the standard he sets for Miss Rand? I, and I think many others, would welcome a demonstration.

PARADOX RESOLVED

It is indeed ironic that Rand should be accused of advocating emotional repression. The struggle for spontaneity and the free expression of emotions dominated, as we have seen, her art no less than her personal life. She recognized that the true individualist has the most to contribute to society, and can benefit the most from being one of its members—another classic Randian paradox. As we have seen, her career was an agonized struggle to confront her alienation from a hostile society. Consider her description of the Halley Fourth Concerto:

> It was a "No" flung at some vast process of torture, a denial of suffering, a denial that held the agony of the struggle to break free. The sounds were like a voice saying: There is no necessity for pain—why, then, is the worst pain reserved for those who will not accept its necessity?—we who hold the love and the secret of joy, to what punishment have we been sentenced for it, and by whom?
> . . . It was her quest, her cry.

So it was. And, after decades of struggle, Ayn Rand, like Dagny Taggart, finally found an answer that satisfied her: the sanction of the victim.

It was Objectivism that led her to the answer. If reason is an absolute, if the good is the rational, then evil is irrational—which means: illogical—which means: unworkable. Evil, being based on contradiction of reality, is inherently self-destructive; left to itself, it must disappear. How, then, can evil even exist?

There can be only one answer: Evil is made possible only by the generous but ill-advised support and assistance, the sanction, of the good. If good people were completely consistent, completely uncompromising, completely intolerant of evil, evil could not endure. Here is the root of a key theme of *Atlas Shrugged*. Rand pitilessly exposes the essence of envy—the hatred of the good for being good. And she exposes altruism as the tool and weapon of evil, the false morality that teaches its victims to hate what is good in themselves.

The discovery of this concept of the sanction of the victim marked, like the renunciation of Nietzsche, a major turning-point in Rand's life and thinking. It changed the way she thought about society—about politics—about her relationships with people. It lay at the root of her attitude toward her enemies— and her attitude toward her supporters. The triumph and tragedy of the Objectivist movement grew out of Rand's conviction that she must deny sanction to evil at all costs.

BEYOND THE TAGGART TERMINAL

It should be evident to the reader that a great deal more could be said about *Atlas Shrugged*. This book is one of the most complex novels ever written, and its analysis poses hundreds of fascinating problems which will occupy scholars for decades.

I lack the space to properly cover the many concepts that Rand developed in this novel: 'sanction of the victim' and the impotence of evil; envy and the hatred of the good for being good; the 'individual surplus' of the great innovators; the intimate connection of philosophical premises and personal and social character; and many others.

Atlas Shrugged is not merely a novel to be read for entertainment, enjoyable though it is. Nor is it a treatise to be read for enlightenment, instructive though it is. The reader will benefit most who regards the book as a sort of magical box full of tightly folded intellectual *origami*, each of which should be carefully opened, contemplated, and cherished.

6 | THE PHILOSOPHICAL PERIOD

The publication of *Atlas Shrugged* in 1957 marked the end of Rand's career as a writer of fiction. During the next decade she devoted herself almost exclusively to the task of extending, elucidating, and publicizing the ideas she had developed. This she did through several media: *The Objectivist Newsletter* and later *The Objectivist*; a series of books collecting her essays from these publications; pamphlets and lectures provided through the Nathaniel Branden Institute. Although much of this material was devoted to political issues (to be discussed in the next chapter), her primary emphasis during this period was on defining Objectivism as a coherent philosophical system, culminating in the publication of a small formal treatise, *Introduction to Objectivist Epistemology*, in 1970.

However, it is a capital error to attempt to fit Rand into the context of academic philosophy. She herself never entered or tried to enter into the world of standard scholarly discourse. She never submitted a paper to a philosophical journal, nor did she even read many such papers—if any.

Rand desperately wanted recognition from other intellectuals, and became angry and depressed when she failed to get it. But if she never achieved the respect of professional philosophers, it was because she was not willing to enter their world or debate on their terms. She was not, nor did she aspire to be, a scholarly or academic philosopher. Yet neither was she a mere popularizer, re-writing and simplifying the ideas of others. Rand fits into a different tradition, that line of active thinkers who have learned from life and speak clearly to any intelligent man or woman.

OBJECTIVISM VERSUS ACADEMIA

Although Rand did not publish professional papers in philosophy, some of her followers have done so. A running debate appeared in the pages of the journal *The Personalist* in the 1970s. Nathaniel Branden and Tibor Machan presented the Objectivist ethics and rights theory, while Robert Nozick was the most prominent of the opposition.[1] To read these arguments is frustrating; the two sides are simply not communicating. The opponents of Objectivism, steeped in the tradition of academic philosophy, display their superior debating skills while adroitly dodging the real issues. There is a tone of rather tolerant amusement, as of a chess-master demolishing a naive opponent. It seems never to occur to them that Objectivists might not regard philosophy as a game.

Ayn Rand stated repeatedly and emphatically that she regarded philosophy not as an academic exercise but as a critical need for every human being. Her interest was in the application of philosophy to the problems of real life. Furthermore, Rand was Aristotelian not only in the content but in the approach and objective of her philosophical thinking. Like Aristotle, Rand regarded it as her task to *help people to know*—to make it possible to find knowledge and certainty. Most modern philosophers have been more attracted to the opposing approach, the tradition of Socrates. They are critical and not uncommonly skeptical, and see it as the duty of philosophy to make people question their beliefs and realize that they know nothing.

Thus academic philosophers, who ought to have been Rand's allies in helping young people to knowledge, proved instead to be her enemies.[2] Philosophy courses, with some honorable exceptions, seem designed to leave students with the impression that philosophy means never having to say you're certain. Young people who seek knowledge to guide them in life are presented with a smorgasbord of contradictory doctrines. Take your choice, they are told—none of them is *really* true. Philosophy does not achieve, and indeed cannot even aspire to, the kind of certainty offered by the sciences.[3]

The traditional dialectical teaching method affects to be neutral among philosophical doctrines. But the dialectical method itself smuggles into the student's mind the doctrines of which it is an expression: That no truth is ever certain, that no question is ever settled, that no argument is irrefutable. All too often the superficial commitment to free inquiry conceals a covert intellectual intimidation. Under the cover of a quest for rigor is conveyed the subtle message that skill at debate makes right. And so everything is uncertain, for perhaps a faster gun will come along tomorrow. It is no accident that the dialectical method of instruction is the normal mode in law schools.

The fact is that teachers of philosophy, in their obsession with critical and analytical skills as opposed to construction and synthesis of knowledge systems, have failed their students. This is not a new criticism. Mortimer Adler—himself a distinguished academic philosopher—saw, and illuminated, the problem in his 1940 essay 'This Prewar Generation'. Following up on his critique more recently, he says:

> Is there any wonder that subjectivism and relativism should have been prevalent among college students exposed to such indoctrination by their professors in the 1930s and 1940s? That indoctrination has continued right down to the present. The moral skepticism among the students is the same as it was then and its cause is the same, though the vocabulary in which it is expressed may have changed in detail.[4]

But the students themselves have not always been so passive as Adler seems to imply. In the NBI era, thousands upon thousands of college students spent evenings in cramped, stuffy rooms listening to tape recordings about philosophy—and paid NBI's not inconsiderable fees for the privilege. Their thirst for knowledge was that intense—a thirst that the universities they were attending during the day failed to satisfy, but Ayn Rand did. It is her focus on substantive problems, her anti-skeptical approach, and her assertion that one can attain knowledge and certainty on fundamental issues, which make her philosophy so attractive to intelligent young men and women. A lot of bright people are turned off by being told that true philosophical understanding means knowing that you know nothing. One might as well sign up for a lobotomy; at current college tuition rates, the surgical route to Socratic insight would be cheaper, too.

Objectivism, with its confident assertion that philosophical problems *can* be solved once and for all—that there are two sides to every question, the right side and the wrong side—is profoundly antithetical to the philosophical tradition of the twentieth century. What's more, Objectivism cuts through or brushes aside many of the field's historical controversies as irrelevant or meaningless. Naturally this does not sit well with most professional philosophers. Objectivists appear to them as dogmatists who casually dismiss the work of famous thinkers without so much as reading it.

Objectivism's distinctive approach and style must be kept in mind as we examine Rand's philosophical thought. Her approach to philosophy, like it or not, was simply not 'scholarly'. Regarding philosophy as too important to be left to the philosophers, she focussed her attention on crucial human problems, especially in ethics, and paid little attention to the more subtle and abstruse issues that concern modern professional philosophers. If, as a result, her thinking has a certain naivety, it also has a certain freshness.

METAPHYSICAL ROOTS

Rand repeatedly expressed her debt to Aristotle for his formulation of the laws of logic and his development of a metaphysics of objective reality. She never attempted to make a significant contribution to metaphysics herself, but adopted the essentials of Aristotelian metaphysics without modification as the basis of her own philosophy. (She rejected, however, Aristotle's cosmology and other peripheral aspects of his metaphysical theories.)

Metaphysics has begun to present a whole series of new problems and challenges with the development of modern science. Some of the most exciting questions deal with, quite literally, 'meta-physics': Why do the laws of physics take the form they do? That is, to what extent, and in what ways, do *a priori* considerations such as self-consistency or causality put constraints on the laws of nature? And what are the implications of modern physics—especially quantum mechanics—for concepts of causality and volition?

Rand paid little attention to these controversies, although many of them had already emerged in the latter part of her lifetime. It seems unlikely that she could have made any contribution to them, in view of her ignorance of mathematics and the natural sciences.

However, Rand contributed a great deal to the popularization of metaphysics. Rand took the viewpoint—by no means universal among philosophers—that philosophy is hierarchical. One's conclusions about metaphysics constrain, if not determine, one's conclusions about epistemology; which in turn constrain one's views on ethics; which in turn constrain one's views on politics and esthetics. She was thus led to place a very strong emphasis on correct metaphysics as the root of philosophical thought.

This emphasis is most obviously evident in *Atlas Shrugged*. Rand's three previous books are very definitely political novels on essentially political themes. *Atlas Shrugged* is a philosophical novel—and more, it is explicitly a novel of metaphysics. At all levels, from its passages of philosophical argument to its symbolism, *Atlas Shrugged* is concerned with the metaphysical roots of ethical, political, and even esthetic choices.

As an Aristotelian, Rand not only asserts the existence of an external, objective reality, but emphasizes that existence is identity. "To exist is to be something." This has the advantage of obviating the need to construct an endless chain of explanations for the universe, for in this viewpoint the 'what' of an existent *is* its 'why'.[5] This underlies Rand's eminently practical approach to philosophical questions. She insists on avoiding intellectual fibrillation by examining philosophical queries for meaning and self-consistency before tackling them. In this way she is able to discard whole libraries of pointless argument and cut through to what is real and important.

AN EPISTEMOLOGICAL RADICAL

Although Ayn Rand was most obviously controversial in her ethical and political views, the case could be made that it was her epistemology that was most radical. What has really driven opposing philosophers up the wall has been less her individualism or her egoism than her claim to certainty. Vital to the structure—and attraction—of Objectivism is its promise of a route to knowledge—real knowledge, certain knowledge. The importance of this attraction is pointed up by the title of Leonard Peikoff's 1989 Ford Hall Forum talk: 'Certainty and Happiness'.

Objectivists have had no difficulty rebutting direct attacks on their claim of certainty. Told, 'Nothing is certain', an Objectivist, like any other Aristotelian, can quickly respond with, 'Are you sure about that?'

Neither do Objectivists have much to fear from the 'How do you know you know?' line of argument. An essay on the subject by Leonard Peikoff [6] takes the position that, once a conclusion is supported by a logical argument, carefully constructed and examined, the burden of proof is on the skeptic. He may not attack it simply by pointing out the possibility of human error; some specific objection must be raised.

Yet, surprisingly, there does not seem to exist anywhere in Rand's writings a definition of 'certainty'. There are a number of questions along this line that Objectivists need to ask themselves. What is certainty, and why does man need it? What does it really mean to say that one is 'certain' of some conclusion? Are there different kinds of 'certainty'? By what criterion can one decide whether some particle of knowledge is certain or tentative? What can one do with certain knowledge that one cannot do with knowledge of which one is merely pretty sure?

Rand, as we have seen, was the ultimate anti-skeptic. In her journal she wrote in 1958, "All the evils of philosophy have always been achieved via epistemology—by means of the 'How do you know that you know?'"[7] The absence of a positive theory of certainty is a striking deficiency in her philosophy.

Though Rand did not take up the question of certainty as explicitly as one would like, she does offer very strong justification for her view that we are capable of knowing reality beyond any reasonable doubt. I want to suggest that she succeeds because she adopts an approach that at first may appear to be merely a matter of style.

For most of this century writings on epistemology have been

permeated with discussions of 'propositions' and 'predicates' and 'logical inference'. Commonly knowledge has been seen as the outcome of a process of *proof*. Ayn Rand's terminology reflects a different viewpoint. She talks in terms of 'concepts', 'abstraction', and 'integration'. Her emphasis is on *understanding*.

Rand obviously acknowledged the role of proof in reasoning; she did, after all, glory in the appellation 'Mrs. Logic'! But she was less interested in how one establishes the truth of particular propositions, than in how one develops a complete structure of interrelated knowledge. Thus her epistemology is centered, not on a methodology of logical inference, but on a theory of concepts.

RAND'S THEORY OF CONCEPTS

The closest thing to a formal, academic paper on philosophy in Rand's work is her mini-treatise, *Introduction to Objectivist Epistemology*. The title, as she indicates at the start of the work, is literal; the book is only an introduction, specifically a discussion of the theory of concepts.

Introduction to Objectivist Epistemology begins with a description of the way in which concepts are formed from percepts. Rand builds a theory of concept-formation based on an analogy with mathematics, in which 'units' and 'measurements' become the raw material for constructing concepts.

This approach leads naturally into a discussion of the Aristotelian structure of definitions in terms of *genus* and *differentia*, corresponding exactly to Rand's theory of concept formation— not surprisingly, as she very likely worked backward from the structure of definitions.

Rand now gets into the real meat of her subject: the question of 'essence' and the debate between 'nominalists' and 'realists'. She pays little attention to issues and distinctions that most philosophers would consider important here. For instance, the term 'nominalist' has actually been applied to a variety of related but distinct positions, as has 'realist'. The question of 'essence' also has a metaphysical component—circles exist (though perhaps no perfect circle), but does 'circularity' exist, and if so what is the manner of its existence? Rand more or less ignores such questions to concentrate on what she sees as the crucial aspect of the problem.

To abbreviate Rand's already simplified summary, the problem may be stated as follows. Is there such a thing as a 'correct' definition for some particular concept? The most commonly held modern view is that there is not; a definition is an arbitrary convenience. This 'nominalist/conceptualist' or Humpty-Dumpty school of thought holds that definitions need only be consistently maintained during a particular discussion. Just as Americans drive on the right side of the road, and British on the left, a concept such as 'bird' may be defined as a feathered animal, or as an egg-laying animal. As long as everyone who is using the definition (or road) agrees to accept a particular procedure, the exact procedure chosen is of no importance.

Opposed to this is the 'realist' school of thought, in its pure Platonic or diluted Aristotelian variants, which hold that there is only one correct definition for a given concept. What, though, could give this 'essence' of the concept its special validity? The 'essence' is real in this view—it actually exists, as a Platonic form or some such entity.

Rand rejects both these approaches. As she describes it, the nominalist regards definitions as arbitrary; there is no 'essence' of a concept. The realist postulates the actual existence of the essence; essence is metaphysical. For Rand, definitions are not arbitrary—there is an essence—but the essence is not metaphysical but epistemological. Though concepts are in the mind, they are not arbitrary because they reflect reality, which is objective.

Now, why should anyone bother with all this? Rand's answer would be that philosophy is practical. The nominalist view assumes that thinking is a matter of detached, abstract debate. It is a game, and the only requirement for the rules is that they be self-consistent and agreed to by all the players.

But for Rand, thinking is man's means of survival, and its rules are absolutely critical. If you pick the wrong way to define a concept, it may not just be 'Well, that's an interesting way to look at the subject'; it could kill you.

The same practical considerations prompt Rand to reject the realist position. Thinking must be contextual. As a practical matter, one cannot wait to learn everything there is to know about a concept, so that one can discover some 'ultimate' essence. Even in the context of limited knowledge, one must have some essence—something to think with, until one learns more.

Take for example the concept 'critical mass'. We all know roughly what this means, but for nuclear physicists, developing an exact definition was, shall we say, critical. When one is working with plutonium assemblies, one cannot afford the casual attitude of the nominalist; one's definition of 'critical mass' had better correspond as exactly as possible to reality. To use an arbitrary definition makes thinking more difficult, and increases the possibility of a mistake in reasoning which may have rather serious consequences. The realist's approach is also defective. The first approach to the concept of critical mass may be primitive—for instance, failing to take into account the dependence on the shape of the object; a sphere of plutonium has a lower critical mass than a cube. But if one waits, avoiding reliance on the concept of critical mass until everything about fission is completely understood, difficulties are likely to mushroom during the early experiments. A concept such as 'critical mass' can be valuable, even essential, to learning, although only imperfectly understood.

Rand's view of essence, one should note, brings her epistemology into line with her metaphysics and her ethics and achieves a uniform consistency in her conception of the human mind. Here, as elsewhere in her work, she decisively rejects the mind-body dichotomy. For Rand, mind is part of reality. In metaphysics, she holds that consciousness is neither illusory, nor a projection of some special, mystical plane of meta-reality; consciousness perceives reality and is part of it. This leads to her conclusion, in epistemology, that concepts, the working fluid of consciousness, are also real—neither arbitrary constructs, nor 'forms' in some meta-reality, but part of ordinary existence. In ethics, Rand's principle leads her to emphasize the complete integration of the human mind and body as the basis of the Objectivist ethics.

Returning to Rand's exposition of epistemology, we find that she goes on to deal with another difficult problem: axiomatic concepts. These concepts—existence, identity, and consciousness—are the broadest possible abstractions. Because they identify the most fundamental aspects of reality and knowledge, no other concept can be formed without use of them. It is in this sense that they are 'axiomatic'.

THE ANALYTIC-SYNTHETIC DICHOTOMY

It should be noted at this point that the Objectivist theory of concepts completely nullifies Kant's 'analytic-synthetic dichotomy'—a sophistry which has confounded and confused generations of college sophomores. A valuable essay on this subject by Leonard Peikoff is appended to Rand's text. Though the Objectivist refutation of the dichotomy is not the only challenge to Kant on this issue, nor even perhaps the most cogent, it is probably the clearest and most easily understood.[8]

Briefly, Kant's distinction divides propositions into two classes: 'analytic' statements, which are, directly or indirectly, true by definition; and 'synthetic' (strictly speaking, 'synthetic a posteriori') statements, which state empirical facts. 'Analytic' statements are 'logically true', but provide no information about reality, since they are in essence just restatements of the definitions of the terms used in them. 'Synthetic' statements, on the other hand, cannot be logically proved; they can only be inferred from what we happen to observe and thus are uncertain, subject to change as we gain new experience. It is therefore impossible for reason to generate knowledge which is both certain and about reality. Kant himself thought that there were 'synthetic a priori' judgments which were built into the human mind and allowed us to know things without the need for experience or reason. This view, however, is not widely accepted; what has achieved immense influence is the use of the analytic-synthetic dichotomy as an argument for epistemological skepticism.

The Objectivist counter to this dichotomy argues that concepts subsume all the characteristics of the entities to which they refer, not just those included in the definition. Thus 'men are rational animals' is no more analytic than is 'men are featherless bipeds'; the latter, as well as the former, can be derived by 'analysis' of the concept. And the former is no less synthetic than the latter, since the definition of man is based on experience and is not arbitrary in the manner of the nominalists.

The analytic-synthetic dichotomy is merely a more subtle formulation of Hume's assertion that neither deductive reasoning nor inductive reasoning can provide us with real—that is, non-tautological and also certain—knowledge. Deductive reasoning, we are told, can prove nothing that is not already implicit in the postulates assumed; inductive reasoning is at best statistical inference and can never be certain in its predictions.

Objectivism simply rejects the dichotomy. Reasoning, for Rand, is a means of comprehending reality. Inductive reasoning derives concepts from observations of facts; deductive reasoning subsumes new instances under known concepts. Like the two blades of a pair of scissors, these modes of thinking do together what neither can do alone.

EPISTEMOLOGY IN PRACTICE

In her closing chapters, Rand surveys a few important practical issues in epistemology. In particular, she attempts to deal with what she regards as an attack on scientific knowledge by the logical positivists. The position she opposes had become the dominant paradigm of scientific epistemology following the 1962 publication of Thomas Kuhn's brilliant and extremely influential book, *The Structure of Scientific Revolutions*.[9] Briefly, this is the view that scientific progress involves a series of 'paradigm shifts', in which an existing theory is gradually overwhelmed by new facts or insoluble problems, forcing development (or acceptance) of a new theory. The older theory, and the concepts on which it is based, are thus invalidated. Kuhn's model has been widely used to attack the very concept of scientific knowledge; according to these Kuhnists—perhaps we should call them 'vulgar Kuhnists'—nothing may be considered certain, for everything we know is subject to reversal by some future 'paradigm shift'. Or, as Rand puts it:

> On such a premise, every advance of knowledge is a setback, a demonstration of man's ignorance.[10]

Rand points out the philosophical roots of this error. She emphasizes that concepts are open-ended and subsume all information about their referents, including that not yet discovered. Thus new facts and unexpected discoveries extend or expand our concepts; they do not invalidate them. Unfortunately Rand passes over this subject quickly; a scientist could wish that she would deal with Kuhn and his followers in more detail, for they have done great damage to scientific epistemology.[11]

Indeed, in general it is regrettable that Rand's ignorance of the sciences left her unable to contribute directly to scientific epistemology. Many of the most crucial modern problems in epistemology are raised by work in the sciences.[12]

If the reader wonders what could constitute a really 'practical' epistemological problem, here is an example. It not infrequently occurs that we must choose between two theories. One theory, let us call it A, is internally self-consistent, but there are some experimental facts that contradict it. The other theory, call it B, is consistent with all the facts but contains internal contradictions. No better theory is currently available, but one must make decisions, and right now—to design a spacecraft, to plan a campaign against a deadly epidemic, to prevent an explosion in a refinery. One must act, and on the basis of one theory or the other. Which should be chosen, A or B? This is an epistemological problem. The solution is left as an exercise for the reader.

THE OBJECTIVIST ETHICS

Rand's most substantial contribution to philosophical thought lies in the field of ethics. It was Ayn Rand who, after 2,000 years of failed attempts, finally proposed a viable solution to the fundamental problem of ethics: deriving normative from factual statements, or, less formally, deriving 'ought' from 'is'.[13] Philosophers have long recognized this as a major problem. Indeed, in the twentieth century most philosophers have despaired of the prospect of developing any sort of logically justifiable ethics. Arguably Ayn Rand's most important accomplishment was producing a solution to this problem. In response, her opponents have concentrated their fire primarily on her ethical reasoning.

I hope, therefore, the reader will forgive me for devoting a great deal of space to this subject. The following discussion will not only present Rand's reasoning, but analyze it in some depth.

I will suggest that the Objectivist ethics can be made more rigorous if certain arguments are reformulated. Then I will compare Rand's approach to Aristotle's and show how she can deal with the moral skepticism of Hume. The various arguments of Rand's critics will be surveyed. Finally, I want to look at the implications of the Objectivist ethics and consider some ways in which it may be extended.

Every human society has had ethical precepts, claims that one 'ought' to do, or not do, certain things. How can such claims be justified? The historic justifications have been such as: 'You ought to, because I say so.' Or: 'You ought to because God, speaking through me, says so.' Or: 'You ought to because all the rest of us took a vote and the majority says so.' Or: 'You ought to because if you don't we'll burn you at the stake.'

At least in modern times we would not accept any of these modes of argument to settle a factual question such as, say, whether the earth revolves around the sun. Why should we accept them in determining moral questions? But if we don't, just how should we determine the truth of a moral dilemma?

Rand attacks the problem of ethics by going to the root, to a question of 'meta-ethics'. Instead of asking, 'Which morality is correct?', she asks, 'Just what *is* a "morality", anyway?' There are many possible moralities which might be correct: Christian ethics, the Ten Commandments, 'Seek the greatest good of the greatest number', 'Do what thou wilt is the whole of the Law', and many others have been asserted. But what do they all have in common? What is a morality?

A morality—any morality—is a set of rules to guide the actions of an individual human being. This—and only this—is what all possible moralities have in common. This is the definition of a morality. (Rand puts it: "A code of values to guide man's choices and actions."[14])

Well, given this, asks Rand, why should there be any morality at all? This is of course a normative question, so let's rephrase it in factual terms: What would happen to a man who practiced no morality?

A man who practiced no morality would be a man whose behavior was guided by no rules at all. Even Alistair Crowley's morality has a rule ('Do what thou wilt') but our hypothetical literally amoral man could not follow even his whims consistently. He would have to behave as if his brain were connected to a random number generator. What would happen to him? He would of course quickly die.

This suggests that the connection between factual and normative statements is man's life. Man needs morality to live. Man ought to do certain things, because they are necessary in order for him to be. He 'is' because he does what he 'ought'.

Now the skeptic might say, 'You are assuming that I ought to choose life—what if I don't?' It is tempting to reply (as, in effect, John Galt does), 'Fine. If you prefer death, shut up and die.' But this is inadequate; it refutes the arguer, perhaps, but not the argument. It is not enough merely to demonstrate that altruism is a morality based on a premise of death. We need to make a positive argument to show that morality must be based on the standard of human life. To my mind Rand's argument for this position is insufficiently rigorous. However, I will assert that her line of reasoning is basically sound and that it can be put on a very strong footing.

Ethics and Values: Two Lines of Argument

Rand defines a 'value' as "that which one acts to gain and/or keep."[15] A value is an object of human action. Thus we might rephrase the fundamental question of ethics as, 'What values or goals ought one to choose?' For a given person in a given context at a given instant, correct ethics must specify some value to pursue. So it is only logical that if we are interested in ethics we ought to examine the concept of 'value' and ask what that concept implies.

The fundamental argument of the Objectivist ethics is the assertion that value (in the ethical sense) is both *practically* and *conceptually* dependent on life. Rand uses two parallel lines of argument for her case.

There is what might be called the 'metaphysical' line: that all values are dependent on life as a practical, metaphysical matter. Rand asserts that only living creatures have, or can have, values. More, she claims that there can be no meaningful values except those which are aimed at the preservation of the individual's life.

But Rand also uses a separate, 'epistemological' line of argument, which relies on use of the 'stolen concept' approach. As has been pointed out by other writers,[16] Rand makes an argument for human life as the standard of ethics which is analogous to the argument for the validity of logic in epistemology. Just as one cannot demand a proof of the validity of logic, since the concept of 'proof' already assumes the validity of logic; so one cannot challenge life as the standard of ethical value, since the concept of 'value' already assumes that one is talking about a living being. In this line of argument, the concept of value is seen as epistemologically dependent on the concept of life.

I am hesitant to lean on the epistemological line of argument because it appears endangered by circularity. Rand's definition of life is "a process of self-sustaining and self-generated action". This sounds very much as though she is implicitly using the concept 'value' to define 'life'. How could one explain "self-sustaining action" without the concept of action to "gain and/or keep" something? But if 'life' is, directly or indirectly, defined in terms of 'value', then in what sense is the latter conceptually dependent on the former?

Let's turn to the 'metaphysical' line of argument for the Objectivist ethics, which is more fully developed. It faces a somewhat analogous difficulty, which however is 'removable', as mathematicians say.

THE RANDIAN ARGUMENT

In line with her usual epistemological style, in Rand's copious writings on ethics she is mostly concerned with building a conceptual framework. She never attempts a formal proof of the basic principle of Objectivist ethics. However, at one point she does outline the basic structure of her argument explicitly.[17] We may summarize the key steps as follows:

    i.   Living beings, and only living beings, have values (goals).
    ii. Man, being volitional, must choose his values.
    iii. Values—goals—may be means to an end, but must lead to some ultimate end. An infinite chain of means leading to no final end would be meaningless and impossible.

iv. Life is an ultimate end, and furthermore it is the only possible ultimate end, the only 'end in itself '.

v. Therefore, the only meaningful or justifiable values a man can choose are those which serve to sustain his life.

The logical inference which leads to the conclusion is sound enough. Premises i., ii., and iii., though occasionally challenged, hardly seem open to serious attack.[18] The fight is over premise iv. Is life an 'end in itself '? And if so, is it the only possible end in itself? To see where the problem arises, we need some background.

ENDS AND ENDS IN THEMSELVES

The classical philosophical tradition in ethics, tracing back to the Greeks, seeks an 'ultimate end' of human action. The argument typically runs as follows:

Consider a goal, alpha. This goal actually is a means to an end, another goal, beta. But beta is itself a means to another goal, gamma, and so on. Can we find some ultimate goal, call it omega, which is an end in itself, not a means to any other end? If we can, and if we can show that every goal is ultimately a means to omega, then we have a basis for ethics.

Suppose, for instance, that we could establish that every human action is aimed at the individual's happiness. We are compelled to assume this proposition in strong form: A person does nothing, and can do nothing, purposeful unless the purpose is to serve his happiness. Even if he thinks he is doing something for other reasons, his real objective is and must be his own happiness. Then ethics reduces to a matter of engineering, so to speak; one need merely determine the most efficient way to serve one's happiness.

The proposed ethical 'end-in-itself ' has been variously identified as justice, love, equality, the greater glory of God, and many other things. But in the end nobody has been able to satisfactorily establish that all goals are means to some end-in-itself.

Has Rand found the answer? It looks problematic at first glance. *Is* life an end-in-itself? Do humans *never* regard life as a means to an end? One thinks of Tony, willing himself to live for one more minute, then one minute more, until he can find someone to carry his urgent warning to Rearden. And is life the *only* end-in-itself? Do humans *never* seek any other value for its own sake? Critics have seen this premise as the crucial weak point of the Randian argument.

Rand's chain of reasoning will not hold unless she can show that, as a matter of metaphysical fact, there is no 'end in itself' other than life. What if there are other ultimate ends, unrelated to, and perhaps even incompatible with, life or survival? Then it will *not* follow that all values must serve to sustain life. So Rand in adopting this argument requires herself to prove a negative.

At best this is going to be difficult, and probably it will be impossible. Take just one prospective counterexample: reproduction. Even with modern medicine a woman faces a noticeable risk of death in having a child. Taking into account economic and other costs, one can scarcely argue that reproduction makes a net contribution to the survival of the parents. It certainly seems plausible to assert that people value their offspring as ends in themselves, and not just as means to the survival of the parents.[19]

Before we can deal with the problem we have identified, we must recognize that Rand is not using the term 'end in itself' in its traditional sense:

> Metaphysically, *life* is the only phenomenon that is an end in itself: a value gained and kept by a constant process of action.[17]

Clearly this is not the usual conception of an 'end in itself'. But just what does it mean, then? Here is a paraphrase by Harry Binswanger: ". . . only life is an action directed toward the perpetuation of itself."[20] And illuminating this in more detail:

> A common misconception is that of thinking of 'survival' as if it were some single vital action that occurs after all the other actions [necessary to life] have been completed. 'Survival', however, means the continuation of the organism's life, and the organism's life is an integrated sum composed of all those specific actions which contribute to maintaining the organism in existence. In this sense in living action the parts are for the sake of the whole: the specific goal-directed actions are for the sake of the organism's capacity to repeat those actions in the future.
>
> An ultimate goal, if it is truly ultimate, must be an 'end in itself'. An 'end in itself' gives the appearance of a vicious circle: it is something sought for

the sake of itself. This circularity vanishes when we regard *life* as an end in itself: actions at a given time benefit survival, which means they make possible the organism's repetition of those actions in the future, being then again directed toward survival, which means their repetition, and so on.[21]

What Rand and Binswanger seem to be saying is that life is an 'end in itself' in an unusual and very special meaning: Life is an ordered collection of activities, which are means to achieving an end, which is—simply those activities. Every action taken to sustain life is simultaneously a means (because it supports life) and an end (because life is by definition simply the collective of such actions).

This conception of life is not only accurate and perceptive, but enormously fruitful for ethics. What's more, it offers a way to escape from the need to prove a negative in the argument for the Objectivist ethics.

THE MEANS TEST

At this point I want to suggest that we can reformulate Rand's argument in a way that leads to the same conclusions, without encountering the difficulty that we discovered above. All we need do is recognize that Rand's idea of 'life' as a sort of self-contained vortex of values which are simultaneously ends and means allows us to reverse the traditional program, as follows.

Consider a goal, Z. Attaining this goal is dependent on another goal, Y, which is a means to Z. Y in turn is dependent on another means, X, and so on. Is there some ultimate *means*, A, which is a means for all other goals? There is indeed: Life is a prerequisite for pursuing any other goal.

We are now in a position to ignore the problem of competing 'ends in themselves'. Let us argue as follows: Man must choose what values to pursue. But can something be a value if its attainment would be such as to eliminate or reduce one's ability to pursue values? To seek an end while rejecting an essential means to that end, is to act (means) to gain and/or keep a value (end) while not so acting—which is a contradiction. So whatever ultimate ends there may be, one can seek them only if, and to the extent that, one values that which serves one's own life.

Whether or not life is the *only* ultimate end, it is an end which is a necessary means to any and all other ends.

The Aristotelian flavor of this approach becomes evident if we phrase the argument this way:

> This goal is a means for all other goals, and not for some special genus apart from others. And all men value it, because it underlies all values. For a value which everyone must hold, who values anything at all, is not arbitrary. Evidently then such a value is the most certain of all; which value this is, let us proceed to say. It is the life of man *qua* man.

To my mind this line of argument offers the prospect of putting the Objectivist ethics on a truly solid logical footing.

RAND AND THE ARISTOTELIAN LEGACY

Jack Wheeler[22] argues that Aristotle anticipated the Randian ethical argument in key ways, and he makes his case well. We need not deny the originality of Rand's accomplishment in conceding, as Wheeler puts it, that she sees farther because she stands on the shoulders of Aristotle. I would take the position, though, that Rand's perception of the crucial connection between values and life is a very major innovation indeed and allows her to ground her ethics solidly in a way which is quite impossible for Aristotle, and indeed for the neo-Aristotelians such as Henry Veatch.

But to fully illuminate certain aspects of the Objectivist argument it is helpful to refer to the opening of the *Nicomachean Ethics*. Aristotle begins his analysis by attacking the question, "What is the good?" After explaining the notion of an ultimate end, the "highest good", he surveys various suggestions for identifying this highest good. Then, to open discussion of his own view, he invokes an analogy.

We understand, says Aristotle, what is the 'good' in the sense of a good physician or a good general or a good carpenter. The 'good' for each of these is the goal of his profession—a healthy patient or a won battle or a well-constructed house. And a 'good' professional is thus one who is effective and skillful in pursuing the end appropriate to his art. If we then ask what is the highest or most general good, to which all humans ought to aspire, it must be to live most fully that life proper to man; and the 'good' man is one who lives this life.

Well, to the modern or post-Hume philosophical mind, this argument depends on a false analogy, a truly stunning non-sequitur. How can we identify 'good' (= 'skillful') with 'good' (= 'moral')? Would we say that a surgeon is morally good simply because he is skillful at his craft? Of course not!

Let's see how Ayn Rand's line of argument can deal with Hume's ethical skepticism. If we look at her reasoning from a certain perspective, we will find that she indeed has done something very similar to what Aristotle did in grounding his ethics. But I will argue that Rand, if not Aristotle, is perfectly sound, and that she can climb into the ring with David Hume with a well-justified confidence.

FROM IS TO OUGHT:
IS THERE AUGHT OR IS ALL FOR NOUGHT?

It is a truism of modern philosophy that statements about 'good' and 'bad', in the moral sense of these terms, differ essentially from ordinary statements of fact. 'Normative' statements, it is said, cannot be proved; they are a matter of personal preference, or social rules, or religious prescription.[23]

It is this truism that Ayn Rand challenges. She asserts that the Objectivist ethical code constitutes a valid, verifiable morality, in which the distinction between 'good' and 'bad' is not arbitrary or intuitive but logically derivable from the facts of reality.

To preview Rand's approach, consider the following response to the Humean argument. The argument may be exemplified by contrasting two statements:

'You are a human being.'
'You ought always to tell the truth.'

Hume's argument says that the first statement is factual, the second normative, and that these two types of statement fall into entirely disjoint categories. Furthermore, there is no way to derive normative statements from factual statements.

This position is superficially plausible, but what happens if we look at it a little more closely? Consider the following statements:

'You ought to format a new disk before attempting to write a file to it.'
'You ought not to open with 1. P–KN4.'
'You ought to first examine the equation to see if the variables are separable.'

To which type do these statements belong? Clearly if they are not normative statements, they are at least phrased as if they were. Yet they are factual statements, and they can be logically derived from observation in the same way as any other factual statement. Thus we see that rules can be factual statements. If expanded, they have the form, 'In order to accomplish X, it is necessary (or at least helpful) to do Y.' In the examples given, X is (respectively) operating a personal computer, winning a game of chess, and solving a first-order, first-degree differential equation.

So, if we can agree on what morality is to accomplish, we can develop moral rules as factual statements. For normative statements are merely factual statements about means and ends.[24] Here is how we can get from is to ought.

But, of course, at this point we will be challenged. We are making precisely the same error that Aristotle made in using the word 'good' in two different meanings. Everybody knows that 'ought' in the operational sense, as we have used it above, does not mean the same thing as 'ought' in the normative, or moral sense of the term. We are simply drawing a false analogy. Who would be silly enough to assert that there is something moral or virtuous about formatting a floppy disk, for God's sake!

But we need not give up at this point. Let us take a bold step. First, though, we must suspend operations for a moment while I resort to another analogy.

Physicists have long known that gravity produces effects similar to those of acceleration. An astronaut in outer space, whose rocket is accelerating at about 10 meters per second squared, will find himself feeling the same sensation of gravity he would experience were he simply standing on the surface of the earth. But of course, in Newtonian times, everybody knew that these two phenomena were not really the same, and that the apparent similarity was merely coincidental. Then Einstein tried making the assumption that the effects of acceleration and of gravity really *are* indistinguishable in every way. The result was the Theory of General Relativity, and experimental test confirmed that Einstein's radical conjecture was indeed correct.

Now Rand does much the same sort of thing, and let us see if we can follow her. Let us simply assert that 'ought' in the operational sense, and 'ought' in the normative sense, are after all equivalent, and challenge the critics to prove that they aren't! For, once Mr. Hume is on the defensive, we see at once that he has a glass chin. If the skeptic agrees that the normative 'ought' is equivalent to the operational 'ought', then the whole problem of 'deriving ought from is' instantly evaporates. If he does not we may ask, just what *is* the meaning of the normative 'ought'? If he invokes tradition or religion, or his emotional feelings about right and wrong, the Objectivist will happily agree that such an 'ought' cannot be derived from 'is'! The skeptic is reduced to saying that the Objectivist ethics isn't 'really' morality, even though it can provide a prescription for any specified moral dilemma. But this is merely to say that if he doesn't agree with the rules, it isn't morality.

So we may now feel that the Objectivist argument has given us a firm footing and that we can get from 'is' to 'ought' by a logical procedure. Morality, we will say, is a process of selecting goals; the appropriate goals are determined by the principle of sustaining human life, based on the facts of human nature—the 'is'; and moral rules—the 'oughts'—merely identify the connections between the ends and the means.

But there is a price to pay for bridging this philosophical chasm. In saying that 'ought' has only one meaning, and not two, we are compelled to defend the proposition that formatting a floppy disk *is* an act of moral significance. In fact, any set of procedures, from the rules of football to a recipe for beef stew, may become part of our structure of morality. This does seem a bit heavy-handed, and hardly in accord with the way we normally think about morality. And since the argument above, as I have presented it, is a very loose paraphrase indeed of Rand's reasoning, one may reasonably ask if her argument is being fairly represented.

A quotation from *Atlas Shrugged* may perhaps indicate whether Rand would care to defend this position. Here is Francisco D'Anconia explaining to Hank Rearden the moral significance of—a steel mill.

> "If you want to see an abstract principle, such as moral action, in material form—there it is. Look at it, Mr. Rearden. Every girder of it, every pipe, wire and valve was put there by a choice in answer to the question: right or wrong? You had to choose right and you had to choose the best within your knowledge—the best for your purpose, which was to make steel—and then move on and extend the knowledge, and do better, and still better, with your purpose as your standard of value . . . Nothing could have made you act against your judgment, and you would have rejected as wrong—as evil— any man who attempted to tell you that the best way to heat a furnace was to fill it with ice."[25]

And when, a couple of pages later, Francisco says, "You knew what exacting morality was needed to produce a single metal nail", the point is driven home. From her books—as well as from her personal behavior—we can deduce that Ayn Rand did regard essentially every human choice as a moral choice, in the most fundamental sense. Consistency, and price no object, was her policy, and here we see it again. It is not an easy way of life into which logic has led her, and one can now more clearly understand the lament of Dr. Stadler:

> "You're asking the impossible! Men can't exist your way! You permit no moments of weakness, you don't allow for human frailties or human feelings! What do you want of us? Rationality twenty-four hours a day, with no loophole, no rest, no escape?"[26]

And indeed that is exactly what Rand wants of us, or rather what she demonstrates we ought to want of ourselves. Her principle unifies thought and life and everything clicks into place. 'Ought' in the operational sense *is* normative ought. 'Good' in the sense of skillful and well-done *is* moral good. 'Right' in the sense of logically correct *is* morally right.[27]

WHAT IS THE MEANING OF LIFE ANYWAY?

We still have one step to take if we are to put the Objectivist ethics on a firm footing. Rand demonstrates that life is the root of all value; but then she goes on to specify the standard of value as "the life of man *qua* man". Somehow we have made a transition from 'life' meaning pure biological survival to "life of man *qua* man" meaning something like Aristotle's good life. When Rand invokes "the life of man *qua* man" as a moral standard, the critic may protest that something other than life (that is, survival) is now being added. Rand's standard may now be characterized as 'biological survival with some added quality'; the critic may demand identification, and justification, of this apparently hazy added quality that makes life the "life of man *qua* man".

Rand's answer is simple: there is no real distinction between the 'simple biological survival' of a human being and the "life of man *qua* man". She applies an Aristotelian metaphysical principle: To exist is to have identity. To survive as a living organism *is* to live the kind of life appropriate to that type of organism. To survive as a man *is* to live the life of man *qua* man. There is no such thing as generic survival which comes in a plain white box and may be taken in combination with any lifestyle one wishes. Reality offers only a package deal: the brand-name product, *LIFE MQM*, is the only box on the shelf.

To survive requires a complex, organized structure of action. A human being cannot survive by acting like a dog, a hippopotamus, or a philodendron. Those strategies are not appropriate to, or effective for our species. Still less can a person survive by using no strategy at all. When a man says, 'I will survive', he is saying, 'I will act as a human being'.

Some difficulties, though, do arise when we try to put Rand's standard into application. Note that Rand will approve of suicide under certain circumstances. In *Atlas Shrugged*, for instance, the Sheriff of Durance says that he will not pass judgment on the man who kills himself because of unbearable suffering. Cherryl Taggart commits suicide rather than live in a world of Jim Taggarts, and Rand expresses no disapproval. John Galt explicitly states his intention to kill himself if Dagny is used against him as a hostage. Can this be consistent with Rand's argument for life as the standard of value? Several of her critics have cited it as a contradiction. If sustaining the "life of man *qua* man" may, under certain circumstances, require one to seek death, then "life MQM" must be a rather peculiar type of life.

Once again we face a real difficulty, but one that can be dealt with. We can resolve the apparent contradiction if we look at Galt's argument with Mr. Thompson. "Don't you want to live?" asks the latter. Galt replies, "I do want to live. I want it so passionately that I will accept no substitute."

Now we are getting to the key. Rand once again is challenging us to look at a fundamental question: What is life? What does it mean to live? Philosophers and scientists have long haggled over the definition of life, but one thing is sure: Essential to every known or conceivable form of life, be it a man, an aardvark, a virus, a Martian, or a sentient super-computer, is goal-directed behavior. And goals imply—indeed by Rand's definition essentially are—values. So there is an ineradicable connection: living beings, and only living beings, have values. Those who have no values, or no possibility of acting to achieve values, are, in effect, dead.[28]

So Galt will kill himself if Dagny is tortured. "There would then be no values for me to seek." Or, as he puts it to Mr. Thompson, "The offer not to kill me is not an inducement." Life is *not* merely the absence of death.

I find this passage suggestive. Rand's writings on ethics tend to present life as a binary, on-off, either-or status of an organism. But this is not really compatible with Rand's concept of life as a complex collection of survival-sustaining actions. I therefore want to propose that we modify the argument slightly.

What is the meaning of 'life'? Consider a steer in the slaughterhouse, a second after it has been killed. A biologist would say, of course, that the animal is dead—as a steer. Yet virtually all of the billions of individual cells in its body are at this point still alive and functioning. Indeed, many cells will still be alive when the ground round arrives in the meat section of the supermarket. So even from the strictest biological point of view there is a sense in which 'life' is more than a binary or 'on-off' attribute.

If life is defined in terms of an organism's exhibition of goal-directed behavior[29] then we must visualize the possibility that it can exist on a multitude of levels. On what we might call the 'hamburger' level, cellular behavior is very primitive, consisting of a small set of rather simple tropisms. The 'warm body' level, in which all or at least some organs are functioning, represents a higher level of complexity. When the organism—a human being, in the case we are concerned with—is able to perceive and to act, then the range of goals accessible to him expands enormously, and it is only at this level that we would regard him as 'completely alive'. And yet, need we stop here? If our subject is more alert, more intelligent, more healthy, more strong, is he not more able to select goals and pursue them, and is he therefore not more alive yet?

It can be confidently asserted that this concept of life is perfectly valid from a biological point of view. Indeed, many of the modern controversies of 'biomedical ethics' are confronted on the shadowy borderland which is now seen to lie between the traditional domains of life and death. It also accords with the way in which we as human beings regard our own existence and that of our comrades. It is a commonplace to regard those dull, lethargic people who seem to have been defeated by the challenges of existence as being less than fully alive. And who has not awakened on a Spring morning, full of zest, and said, 'Ah, I feel very alive today!'

We can now see that life should be regarded not as a discrete but as a continuous quantity. If one increases one's values and one's ability to attain them, one actually becomes more alive. If one decreases one's options, one becomes less alive. A healthy person is more alive than a Karen Ann Quinlan. A free man is more alive than a slave. And above all, a moral man is more alive than an immoral man. I therefore suggest that we reformulate Rand's argument: morality consists not just of preserving life (MQM), but of maximizing life (MQM).[30] The objective of ethics is not simply to maintain one's ability to pursue values, but to optimize it.

Let's recapitulate. The Objectivist ethics may be seen as a set of rules to guide human action, which is based explicitly on maximizing life. Any 'anti-Objectivist ethics', which chooses values hostile to life, then must be self-contradictory because it would involve destroying or eliminating values by attacking that which makes values possible. Furthermore, the acceptance of anti-life 'values' contradicts the basis which makes the concept 'value' meaningful. Any 'non-Objectivist ethics', which chooses values neither favorable nor hostile to life, may be challenged to give a cause for its selection of such values.

THE OBJECTIONS TO OBJECTIVIST ETHICS

The Randian argument in ethics is nothing if not controversial, and it has come under heavy attack from philosophers. The most effective criticisms are those which either attack Rand's 'ultimate end' premise or exploit the concept of life as 'pure survival'. As I have pointed out above, these objections are cogent but can be met effectively by modifying the Randian argument in ways that do not affect its basic structure or its conclusions.

Various other criticisms of the Objectivist ethics have been raised in both formal and informal venues. Let's briefly survey them.

SIMPLE MISREPRESENTATIONS

A number of critics have asserted that the Objectivist ethics is simply a disguised or variant form of Thrasymachan or Nietzschean or Stirnerian 'might makes right' egoism, or even that Rand advocates some sort of Nazi-like attitude. Sometimes real or alleged deficiencies in Rand's personal conduct are cited to suggest that she displayed such behavior in practice as well as advocating it in theory. Some characterize Objectivism as identical to Social Darwinism, generally depicting the views they dislike in terms that indicate that they have read nothing from either school of thought. Since such assertions don't address the real nature of the Objectivist ethics in the first place, it is neither possible nor desirable to answer them.

FROM LEAKING LIFEBOATS TO THE ASTEROID TEST

It used to be fashionable to attack Objectivists with 'lifeboat dilemmas'. 'Suppose you are on a lifeboat and the only way to survive is to murder your companion . . .' As Rand has pointed out, by assuming a situation so far from the normal human condition, one has invalidated the 'normal' prescriptions of Objectivist ethics.[31] At this point we have moved outside the context for which the ethics was constructed. One can still have an Objectivist ethics—one can still try to maximize one's life—but the specific rules would change. In fact, since an emergency may be defined as a situation inherently hostile or dangerous to human life, the first rule of emergency ethics would be 'Take action to end the emergency!' So any such exceptional cases may be regarded as rare, temporary, and unimportant to the real task of ethics. Incidentally, it should be noted that in real-life emergencies the 'push the other guy out of the lifeboat' technique is seldom if ever advisable. Historical examples show that those who survive do so by co-operating with their comrades in misfortune, not murdering them.

Another challenge along the same lines is the 'invulnerable criminal dilemma'. 'Suppose you knew for sure that you could get away with robbing a bank. Why not do it? It would be selfish.' This is a little more subtle. The essential answer is that ethics demands not only attaining values at the range of the moment, but maximizing one's ability to attain values in the long run. Go back again to Rand's fiction. There is a continual stress laid on the importance of what one *is* rather than what one *has*. The hypothetical invulnerable bank-robber is unselfish; he diminishes his capabilities by wasting time and effort (if nothing else) on non-productive work; he diminishes his options by putting other people in power over him (since he must lie, at least, to conceal his crime). And of course, in reality—as opposed to some imaginary universe—bank robbery is a distinctly hazardous affair.

Eric Mack claims that Bertrand Russell was immoral by Objectivist standards and therefore "has been a problem for disciples of Rand" because he lived to a very ripe old age.[32] This is invalid even by the most literal interpretation of Rand's wording. Suppose, in fact, that pure survival were to be the ethical criterion. Ethics would then tell us, for instance, 'cross a street only with the "walk" light'. Now, statistically, those who obey this rule will live longer, but one could certainly find examples of those who consistently jaywalk and get away with it! Russell was lucky, that's all.

This in fact illustrates an important point: Rand was very much aware that life is, so to speak, a stochastic achievement test. Sometimes the moral person, in spite of all efforts, will encounter a run of bad luck, fail, and die. Sometimes the evil person will encounter a run of good luck and prosper to a ripe old age. No matter how rational or intelligent one may be, one cannot always attain certain knowledge of the consequences of one's actions. (It is partly for this reason that Rand so strongly emphasizes the difference between irrational behavior, which is immoral, and action based on an error of knowledge, which is not.) This uncertainty, which is an inherent part of life, does not change the principles of moral action. The race is not always to the swift, or success to the rational—but that's the way to bet.

Again, Mack asserts that a "looter" is not necessarily likely to live less long than a productive man, so the choice of productivity is only a matter of taste. Is it? The looter is a parasite. He destroys or at least damages his victims. Every time he is 'successful', he reduces his future opportunities. The productive man, after each success, is richer not just in wealth, but in experience, skill, and knowledge, better equipped to succeed next time. Instead of victims wary of further attack, he faces partners and customers eager to do business with him again.

And is it true that looters do well? Have the thugs of totalitarian states led, on average, long lives? The fact is that for every Deng who lives into old age, there are dozens of Berias and Roehms and Trotskys who fail in the struggle for power and meet with untimely and unpleasant ends.

It's instructive here to take one more example, which archetypically illustrates this general line of argument. This is a case by David Friedman[33] which is aimed, not specifically at Objectivism, but at any attempt at moral grounding for human rights. Friedman postulates the following moral dilemma:

*The earth is going to be destroyed tomorrow by an asteroid strike (!)

*This can be prevented by use of a piece of equipment costing $100 (!!)

*Of which there happens to be only one unit in existence (!!!)

*And the owner refuses to let go of it because he'd just as soon
he and the rest of the human race were killed (!!!!)
So: Should one or should one not steal it?

Here we have a real beauty, almost a caricature of this
sterile mode of ethical argumentation. It brings out very explicitly
the essence of this approach: to attack the Objectivist ethics by
saying, 'But suppose reality weren't what it is? Then your rules
would get you in a mess.' The Objectivist reply is simply, 'So
what?'

The Objectivist ethics is based on a context of the full reality of
human life. Human beings—real human beings—are not hypothetical constructs who can somehow live and thrive by cheating,
theft, and murder. And in fact, when it's not Rand who is saying
this, the statement isn't even controversial. 'The wages of sin is
death.' 'Crime doesn't pay.' 'Evil deeds do not prosper.' The
contrary is difficult even to imagine. Writers of fiction reward
their heroes and punish wrongdoers, not just as moral propaganda, but because it's hard to make the reverse believable.
Could even the talent of Dostoyevsky make us believe in a
Raskolnikov who gets away clean and lives happily ever after?

Well, some philosophers will defend—or at least affect to
defend—the proposition that crime does pay. They assert that it
really is in the self-interest of at least some people to live as
parasites and seek values by the destruction of other people. At
this point, though, we may sign off, because we have left the
realm of pure philosophy. The practicality of crime as a mode of
life need not be a subject of speculation or analysis; it can be,
and has been, and is studied empirically. Most of us know what
conclusions result.

THE GALT-LIKE GOLFER

King invokes a somewhat more subtle dilemma to attack the
Objectivist ethics.[34] What about a highly productive man who,
rich at 30, retires and spends the rest of his life playing golf?
Has he really done anything wrong? Yes, he has, by the standards of Objectivist ethics. Again, it's not what he has that
counts, nor even what he does, but what he is. By living in idle-

ness, he is diminishing his productive capacity and ability, and thus acting against his own life. In reality skills decline if not practiced—business skills, not just golf! Knowledge is forgotten or becomes obsolete if not used; ability and ambition decay if not presented with new challenges. And that matters, because—in reality—fortunes are vulnerable to inflation, depression, and confiscation.

This and many other objections to the Objectivist ethics fail to understand an essential principle involved. We are accustomed to thinking in terms of one of the two moral modes basic to Western culture. The Judaic ethical mode is legalistic; you are good or bad based on what you do. The Jew has made a covenant—a contract—with God. He has merely to live up to its terms to be good. The Christian ethical mode puts actions in second place, and judges you by what you think. Under Christian morality your actions are of secondary moral importance, and it is your intentions and even emotions that determine your moral stature. This is exemplified by the well-known warning that 'lust in your heart' is sufficient to make you guilty of adultery.

Objectivism takes an entirely different approach. Rand utterly rejects the Christian conception. One need not feel guilt over thoughts or feelings. "There are no evil thoughts except the refusal to think." Neither can one take credit for good intentions not carried out in action. "If one of my blast furnaces goes down, can I keep it going by feeding your intentions into it?" But Rand also refuses to wholly accept the Judaic approach. Although Objectivist ethics characterizes actions as right or wrong, the morality of actions is secondary. To Rand, it matters not what you intend, and only indirectly what you do; the real moral essence is what you are—what kind of person you choose to be.

ROBERT NOZICK VERSUS THE COUNT OF MONTE CRISTO

No philosophical disputation would be complete without an example of the classic meaning-switch cheapo, and in the debate over Objectivist ethics Robert Nozick has provided the most ingenious application of this traditional technique.[35]

Nozick asserts that one cannot derive an ethics from the fact that life is a prerequisite for all other values and cites a counter-example: Being cured of cancer is obviously a value. But having cancer is a prerequisite for being cured of cancer. Does this mean that having cancer is a value?

Well, let us take this sophomore stumper in the spirit in which it is intended and have some fun with it. A dedicated dialectician could dance a pleasant polka with Nozick by taking the affirmative of the question. For instance: Who has not on some occasion abstained from eating before a special meal, in order that hunger may sharpen the appetite and the enjoyment? Perhaps we should go all the way with the Count of Monte Cristo. He asserted that nobody could know true joy who had not experienced the ultimate depths of suffering, and went so far as to let a friend think his fiancée had died so he would be really happy when he learned she hadn't. A professional philosopher no doubt could convince us that it really does make sense to beat your head against a brick wall in order to enjoy the sensation when you stop.

But we must be moving on. Let's point out that Nozick has dropped the context that gives meaning to the value he is invoking. 'Being cured of cancer' is a value only to someone who has cancer. Modern cancer cures range from unpleasant to devastatingly painful; nobody would consider the cure a value in itself.

In short, there is an obvious distinction, which Nozick is fogging, between the circumstances which make something a value, and the means used to attain that value. When we say that Philosophy 101 is a prerequisite for Philosophy 102, we mean that the student will need the information, concepts, and skills taught in the first course in order to profit from the second. We may also say that a certain amount of ignorance of philosophy is a 'prerequisite' for Philosophy 102, in the sense that if the student already knows the material he won't benefit from taking the course—but now we are using 'prerequisite' in an entirely different meaning of the term.

Having covered the significant objections to Rand's basic ethical argument, let's consider what she concludes from it.

HUMAN NATURE AND ITS CONSEQUENCES

Rand adheres to a biocentric approach by examining the essential attributes of human nature. She asks in effect (to use modern biological terminology), 'What is the ecological niche of *Homo sapiens*?' Put this way, the answer is clear: Man is the animal that lives by its mind.

Human beings live, not by sharpness of tooth or sharpness of claw, but by sharpness of mind. In a way, biologists make a mistake when they classify humans as mammals; we differ from other mammals so greatly in mode of existence that humans might well be considered to be, like the first proto-amphibian that crawled up out of the sea, representatives of a new class of vertebrate. The possession of the ability to think in concepts and to communicate these concepts to other members of our species is a fundamental difference from other living creatures; it is comparable to the development of wings by birds, or of warm blood by mammals.

Since man's mind is his biological means of survival, the first and most fundamental of the cardinal virtues of Objectivism is rationality. The human mind is the primary tool by which a man is enabled to pursue values, and therefore its application and development is a very primary value. Now, again, it is critical to understand that 'rationality' is a virtue which must be defined in a very broad sense. The casual reader of Rand's nonfiction often receives the impression that rationality is simply a matter of choosing to 'focus' one's mind—or making decisions based on logic, rather than being ruled by emotional whims. This is correct as far as it goes, but inadequate. Rationality in its fullest sense is maximization of one's ability to think, as well as the fullest possible use of this capability in solving life's problems.

Another distinctive characteristic of the human species is its dependence on productivity. The vast majority of plant and animal species exist essentially as consumers, by pure exploitation of their environments. A few species make significant modifications of the environment to create resources for themselves; for instance, beavers dam streams to create ponds in which to live. Through most of its existence, the human species has existed as hunter/gatherer bands, differing in degree but not much in kind from beavers. Modern man, however, operates on a vastly larger scale, making massive changes in his environment to make it suitable for himself. He no longer exists by simple exploitation of existing resources, but by the creation of resources. This way of life, though it has its own special perils, is immensely more successful than the primitive mode. In terms of the Objectivist ethics, the pursuit of values by creation ('production') is infinitely more efficient than simply picking things up. And the higher the scale of capitalization that can be achieved, the more efficient the production is. Productivity, like rationality, is a prime Objectivist virtue because it increases one's options and one's ability to pursue values.

Rand selects as the third cardinal virtue of Objectivism 'pride'. In doing so, she makes explicit the crucial importance she attaches to improving one's abilities and options. There are no less than eight definitions of 'pride' in the Objectivist literature, but primary is: "moral ambitiousness".[36] Nathaniel Branden[37] amplifies this: "Moral ambitiousness, the dedication to achieving one's highest potential, in one's character and in one's life." Thus 'pride' for the Objectivist denotes a constant effort to improve oneself. This translates to a concentration on increasing one's capabilities. The Objectivist must not only be competent; he must make a commitment to self-education and self-improvement, to the constant expansion of his competence to deal with reality.

We need not go any further into the details of the Objectivist ethics. Once one accepts the reasoning so far, the rest follows with little difficulty.

THE ETHICS OF THE FUTURE

Rand's development of the Objectivist ethics was, in its practical significance, her greatest and most lasting intellectual accomplishment. Our generation, and the future generations of mankind, owe her an enormous debt for the guidance she has provided.

Yet there is much work yet to be done in the extension of the framework Rand constructed. There are major gaps in Rand's prescriptions for human behavior. She has almost nothing to say,

for instance, about ethical questions in man-woman relationships, marriage, and raising children. Partly, of course, this reflects her own lack of personal experience with family life. But,
intellectually, it results primarily from her acceptance of the
doctrine of biological plasticity of human beings.

The famous 'nature versus nurture' argument of the twentieth century left its mark on Rand's thought. In rejecting
Nietzsche, she rejected the notion that the abilities, character, and
unique personality of a human being are hereditary in origin.
Thus she makes a particular point in *Atlas Shrugged* of showing a
James Taggart springing from noble stock, of Ragnar Danneskjold
arising from a decadent line, of John Galt appearing from undistinguished lineage in the boondocks of Ohio. Emotionally,
Rand never quite lost her respect for aristocratic bloodlines;
consciously and rationally, she emphatically rejected it.

Yet Rand only partially accepted the counter-trend of en-
vironmental determinism. Ethically and politically, she rejected
the idea that you are what you're taught, that you are a product
of your environment, which determines your thoughts, your
character, and your ability. But—though Rand vigorously
attacked Behaviorism and the related ideologies of environmen-
tal determinism, she accepted the error which lies at their root:
the idea that human beings are born *tabula rasa*, 'blank slates',
with no inherent characteristics.

This error underlies her inability to deal with major ethical
issues involving the sexes and children, and her confusion on such
issues as feminism. If we are born formless minds, blank slates
on which our personalities are written (whether by our culture or
by our wills), if biology has nothing to say in defining the sexes
or creating individual differences, how can a biocentric ethics
give us guidance? Further, if we have no 'instincts' or inherent
biological need to reproduce, why go to the trouble and expense
of having children at all?

During the last decade of Rand's life, the scientific basis for
a full expansion of the Objectivist ethics began to be built. The
new field of 'sociobiology', though starting from biology rather
than philosophy, converges on the same goal Rand pursued:
describing how human ethical values can be explained by, and
derived from, the distinctive biological nature of human beings.

Going beyond primitive notions of 'nature versus nurture', sociobiology attempts to construct an integrated view of man, in which the mind-body dichotomy is rejected. This discipline promises to provide empirical data, and to some extent a theoretical framework, for 'biocentric' moral rules that could contribute in a major way to the future development of the Objectivist ethics.

FROM THEORY TO HOW-TO

Nathaniel Branden has pointed out the need for something beyond ethics as traditionally conceived. It is not enough, he suggests, to develop a set of rules for action, to tell people *what* they ought to do. Ethics is not complete until it provides rules or prescriptions to advise people *how* to be moral. Most of us know the difference between right and wrong—but do we always do what is right? Branden calls for a field of study that would extend ethics into 'how-to' methodology for people who want to be moral.

Naturally psychotherapy or psychology is a logical candidate for this field of, so to speak, para-ethics. (Indeed, Branden's original 'Objectivist psychotherapy', which he has since repudiated, was characterized in exactly these terms.) Most moralists have been inclined simply to rely on human will-power (supplemented by reward and punishment), and thus have not much to contribute. Unfortunately, psychologists have not to date contributed much more. Traditionally they have been prone to assume that if the patient only understands the roots of his behavior he will change it. As Arthur Koestler pointed out in *Arrival and Departure*, this theory doesn't work. Nathaniel Branden (along with a few other psychologists, notably Alexander Weinberg) deserves a great deal of credit for not only raising this issue, but making an effort to develop some useful techniques.

OBJECTIVIST ESTHETICS

Rand attempted to do for esthetics what she did for ethics: put the field on a firm logical foundation, and make it possible to make esthetic judgments on the basis of objective standards. In this task she was only partly successful.

Rand defines art as, "a selective re-creation of reality according to the artist's metaphysical value-judgments". Rand does not attempt to connect esthetics to ethics. Though she does not hesitate to evaluate a work of art as being good or bad in ethical terms, for Rand 'good art' or 'bad art'—esthetic judgment—is not ethical in basis but metaphysical. "The basic purpose of art is not to teach but to show."[38]

The Objectivist esthetics is thus organized into three subdivisions: 1. The nature and purpose of art, and how it is related to metaphysics on the one hand, and human psychology on the other hand. 2. The ethical evaluation of art, which for Rand boils down to the conflict between Romanticism and Naturalism. 3. The esthetic evaluation of art, which is a matter of judging effective craftsmanship and technique.

Absolutely central to the Objectivist esthetics is the notion of 'sense of life'. This is the individual's subconscious view of the nature of the universe and life. It expresses itself in terms of 'metaphysical value-judgments'. Unlike ethical value-judgments, metaphysical value-judgments refer not to evaluations of good and bad but to evaluations of important and not-important. Is challenge important or is safety important? Is success important and failure merely an occasional nuisance—or is it the other way around?

The creator of a work of art expresses his sense of life—or at least a sense of life. Barbara Cartland expresses the sense that romantic love is all-important; Stephen King that fear and horror are fundamental to existence; Mickey Spillane that conflict and violence are the essence of life. Horatio Alger expresses the sense that justice is ultimately decisive in human affairs; Jean-Paul Sartre that it is not. These are the metaphysical judgments of one-dimensional writers; the judgments of Jane Austen, or Victor Hugo, or Ayn Rand, could not be so briefly summarized.

How is a sense of life projected by a work of art? Rand's approach is epistemological: Just as a concept is formed by dropping the concrete examples and retaining the essence which characterizes them, art expresses the creator's sense of life by dropping that which he regards as unimportant and retaining only the important.

According to Rand, the reader or viewer or listener responds to art on the basis of the level of agreement between his sense of life and that of the artist. This seems open to challenge; many people deliberately choose art which expresses the sense of life they would like to have, rather than the sense of life they do have. Consider Ayn Rand herself. Rand's sense of life, as projected in her novels, is one of a world in which men can accomplish great things, but only by means of a violent, tortured struggle against desperate odds. Yet in her own esthetic tastes, exemplified by her choice of music, she sought a sense of life which was free of all challenge or threat, pure undiluted happiness.

The ethical component of art, for Rand, is expressed most clearly in the conflict between the 'Romantic' and 'Naturalistic' schools of art. By her definition: "Romanticism is a category of art based on the recognition of the principle that man possesses the faculty of volition." Naturalism, in contrast, is the esthetic expression of determinism.

Thus Romantic art exhibits certain characteristics: ethical themes, since volition implies choice which implies a potential for moral conflict; strong plot, since volition implies purposeful action; larger-than-life characters, since volition implies values.

Connected to this view of Romanticism is Rand's adoption of a principle from Aristotle: that fiction is more important than history, for fiction can show men and events as they ought to be, rather than as they are.

Rand cautions that esthetic judgment, literally defined, is not a matter of evaluating an art work's sense of life, nor its ethical content. She instead asserts that esthetic judgment should be purely technical: How effectively does the creator express the sense of life and the theme of his work?

In the field of esthetic technique, Rand deals only with the area of literature, which perhaps is not surprising. She provides, as one would expect, some superb insights into the writing process.

Esthetic Difficulties and Definitions

Certainly anyone who is interested in esthetics on any level should read Rand's essays on the subject in their entirety and give them careful study. Her analyses are permeated with deep insight and useful ideas. Yet though she makes a major contribution to the field, Rand's esthetics presents some serious problems.

Ayn Rand's views on the esthetics of music are symptomatic of serious confusion. Anyone who can assert that Beethoven had a "malevolent sense of life", or that Wagner "destroyed melody"[39] clearly cannot be relied on as a guide to musical evaluation. To be fair, Rand herself never claimed (at least in print) that she possessed an esthetic theory for music, and indeed explicitly conceded that she was unable to present such a theory.

This is not surprising, for if one accepts Rand's definition of art, it is not clear how music can qualify. It scarcely seems to be a "representation of reality" in the sense that the definition is used for literature or the visual arts.

This leads us further: What of non-representational art in general? 'Modern' (non-representational) painting and sculpture challenge the Objectivist esthetics also. Are they not art? Certainly not by Rand's definition. Many people, including myself, would say that non-representational paintings are not important art, that they might better be classed as decoration. Even so, they can convey a sense of life, albeit only in a mild and very generalized form.

Rand indeed deals briefly with the decorative arts[40] and in effect (though she does not say so explicitly) seems to regard them as a 'borderline case'.

How about dance? Rand interprets dance as a 're-creation' of human body movements, capturing the grace and fluidity by omitting the unessential.[41] This is perhaps acceptable when discussing, say, ballet; but when we consider Rand's favorite variety—tap dancing—it is rather less satisfactory.

These problems arise because Rand's definition of art is fundamentally flawed. It violates an important principle of epistemology: Every man-made entity is properly defined in terms of its function.

Consider, for instance, the concept 'table'. The naive approach is to define a table as an object with a horizontal flat surface and legs. But this does not capture the essence of the concept. What unites all tables is not their size or shape but their function. We can see this from our own cognitive behavior. If I show you a piece of furniture with four legs, a flat surface, and a small drawer beneath it, and ask what it is, your answer will likely depend on the context of use. If it is sitting in the living room and has a vase with flowers on it, you'll call it a table. If it is sitting in an office and has a computer on it, you'll call it a desk.

Applying this principle to art leads us to a better definition. To begin with, it is certainly true that all art is man-made; a painting of a landscape may be art, but not the landscape itself. There is our genus. What is the function of art? Note that when we speak of function, we mean the purpose from the point of view of the user. For what purpose do we use art? What we seek from a work of art is to be induced to feel an emotion—specifically, a sense of life. There is our differentia. Thus the correct definition of art is: A man-made object or process the function of which is to induce a sense of life in the observer.

Though this definition does not immediately lead to an esthetics of music, it at least does not make the problem more difficult, as Rand's does.

7 | THE POLITICAL PERIOD

A yn Rand, like any rational person, wanted nothing more from politics than not to have to be concerned with the subject. But from childhood she was confronted with the great political issues of the twentieth century, and in her work she could not avoid dealing with them. Rand's radical individualism inevitably made her one of the most controversial political thinkers of her time. She wrote copiously on political problems, in both her fiction and non-fiction work. She even spent a couple of stints as a political activist. Even so, she was never truly a political philosopher, in that she never seriously grappled with the fundamental problems of political theory.

A POLITICAL ODYSSEY

The starting point for Ayn Rand's political journey was her fervent anti-Communism, born of personal experience. She emphasized, quite correctly, that *We the Living* was an anti-collectivist novel, an attack on the totalitarian vision as such, rather than merely Soviet Russia or Bolshevism. Even so, it is notable that she never had much to say about Naziism; much as she opposed it, it seems never to have inspired her with the same visceral hatred that she felt for Communism.

During the 1930s and 1940s the cause of freedom was at low ebb politically and especially intellectually; the dominant ideologies of the day were communism, socialism, and fascism. In American practical politics, the New Deal prescribed taking these collectivist toxins in homeopathic doses to prevent a more serious outbreak. It was in this hostile environment that Ayn Rand fought her first political values.

She began as a political naif, even voting for Roosevelt in 1932. Though the exigencies of survival during the Depression left little time for the struggling writer to spend on inessentials, Rand conscientiously studied economics, conservative political theory, and current events. Even so, she remained innocent enough to become an enthusiastic supporter of Wendell Willkie's 1940 presidential bid. Rand and her husband lived off their savings for months as they worked full time in the Willkie campaign.

The U.S. presidential election of 1940, perhaps more than any other of this century, revolved around major, fundamental issues. In domestic policy, there was the potential for a referendum on the New Deal and the 'mixed economy'. The question of America's entry into World War II was prominent, and even in 1940 it could be seen that intervention would probably imply, in the end, at least a *de facto* alliance with the Soviet Union. Finally, Roosevelt's quest for a third term, following on his scheme to pack the Supreme Court, suggested the danger of a major weakening of constitutional protections. Certainly if there was ever a need— or an excuse—for political involvement, this election was the time for it.

Willkie sought the Republican presidential nomination along the traditional path—the Right. He appeared to many, including Rand, as a crusader for capitalism and traditional American freedoms. Joining his campaign, Rand quickly graduated from typist to propagandist, setting up an 'intellectual ammunition bureau' to assemble arguments against Roosevelt. Then through sheer merit she moved up to public speaking, in spite of her nearly impenetrable Russian accent.

But Willkie, once he had the nomination, followed the customary Republican strategy of 'moving to the center' for the general election. As he compromised one after another of the ideals he had pretended to stand for, Rand became increasingly disillusioned. Though she stuck it out to the end of the campaign, Willkie's support melted away and he lost the election.

In the aftermath, the New Deal was consolidated and even tended by wartime controls, with the government gaining unpre edented powers over the economy. A series of important court precedents irreparably breached important bulwarks set up in the constitution. And the war resulted in a world in which a nuclear-armed Communist empire presented a threat far greater than Hitler ever had.

A handful of right-wing intellectuals clung to one another in the resulting environment like survivors of a shipwreck. Among them for a while was Ayn Rand. Her participation in the Willkie campaign brought Rand into contact with a number of important conservative and libertarian thinkers: Albert J. Nock, Isabel Paterson, Rose Wilder Lane, and others. Disillusioned with politicians, Rand attempted to organize the intellectuals. Her grand scheme quickly disintegrated, as she found them timid, defeatist, and philosophically ungrounded.

Rand became friendly with Isabel Paterson, author of *The God of the Machine*, in spite of fundamental philosophical differences, particularly over religion. Rand learned much about history and politics from Paterson, but eventually the relationship broke up. Ironically, the precipitating cause was Paterson's offensive behavior to some of Rand's other conservative friends. Barbara Branden's account[1] shows Ayn Rand in a novel role as conciliator; it is amusing to watch Rand playing the nervous hostess, desperately trying to keep the volatile Paterson from fighting with her fellow guests.

Rand also met during the 1940s Henry Hazlitt and Ludwig von Mises. After her move to California, Rand became known as an outspoken anti-collectivist; she even testified before HUAC on communist influence in Hollywood. But as she began work on *Atlas Shrugged*, Rand developed her unique philosophy and politics and increasingly distanced herself from the conservative movement. The latter was beginning to recover and grow, nourished by the outbreak of the Cold War. In spite of her fervent anti-Communism, Rand could not join in a movement which, she now saw, was based on a foundation not only different from, but fundamentally incompatible with, her own philosophy.

THE RADICAL FOR CAPITALISM

Rand's break with conservatism became clearly mutual with the publication of *Atlas Shrugged* in 1957. Conservatives abhorred much of her doctrine—the rejection of religion, the call for pure laissez-faire, and the repudiation of altruism and traditional ethical values. What's more, her open advocacy of "selfishness" threatened to discredit the movement and supply ammunition to its enemies. It became important to the conservative intellectual leadership to destroy Rand, or at minimum to repudiate her as a conservative.[2]

William F. Buckley, editor of *National Review*, assigned the book to communist-turned-Quaker Whittaker Chambers. Chambers reviewed *Atlas Shrugged* with a viciousness that surpassed the efforts of even the most virulent liberal critics. In scarcely disguised phrases he portrayed Rand as a Nazi, likening her to the SS monsters who perpetrated the Holocaust—an accusation calculated to maximally offend a Jew. Rand never forgot this libel; and her enemies on the Right, in accord with the principle that one never forgives those one has wronged, pursued her with relentless hate.

THE GOLDWATER DEBACLE

In spite of her intellectual distaste for conservatism, and her personal distaste for Buckley and his minions, Ayn Rand continued to back conservative candidates. In the *Objectivist Newsletter* of October, 1963, Ayn Rand advised her readers to register as Republicans and vote in the presidential primary elections for Barry Goldwater. She based this advice primarily on the need to prevent "an intellectual coup d'état" by Nelson Rockefeller— a takeover of the Republican Party by welfare-state liberals. Her endorsement of Goldwater was tentative, though she cited his position on Cuba and his opposition to the Nuclear Test Ban Treaty as encouraging.

A few months later (March, 1964) Rand endorsed Goldwater more strongly, explaining that "Freedom is his major premise." She described him as "singularly devoid of power lust".

One of the longest articles Rand ever published in the *Objecti-*

vist Newsletter was '"Extremism" or The Art of Smearing' (September 1964). Provoked by the furor over Goldwater's refusal to repudiate the support of the John Birch Society, this essay analyzed the controversy at the Republican Convention in epistemological terms. Rand introduced the idea of the "anti-concept", a useful tool in understanding political propaganda. Terms such as 'extremism' (or 'isolationism' or 'McCarthyism'), she pointed out, are designed to fog out and obliterate real concepts, such as conservatism. She congratulated Goldwater on his handling of this attack.

But by October, Rand was sounding a warning to her students, predicting that Goldwater would likely be defeated because "his campaign has been conducted so badly".

If Rand still retained any hope of a Goldwater victory at this late date she was far behind other political analysts. All but the blindest of Goldwater's partisans had written off his chances even before he was nominated. Still, many of the Objectivist movement's younger adherents had campaigned for him enthusiastically. They needed an explanation.

The December, 1964 issue of the *Objectivist Newsletter* carried an article which had crucial influence on the course of the Objectivist movement—and, perhaps, on the course of American politics. Entitled 'It Is Earlier Than You Think', this essay reaffirmed Rand's analysis of the Goldwater campaign. She ascribed his defeat to the lack of any rational intellectual basis for conservative ideas. Rand went on to assert that the debacle had at least cleared away the old-guard conservatives, leaving the way clear for consistent supporters of capitalism to fight more effectively. But Rand warned that it was too early for direct political action. Instead, she urged her supporters to work in the intellectual sphere: "The battle has to be fought—and won—in colleges and universities, before it can be carried to the voting booths."

This article began a period in which the Objectivist movement became, quite explicitly and self-consciously, hostile to the very idea of political action. Those who were unwilling to renounce activism were read out of the movement. There was an indirect effect on the conservative movement also. The youth wing of conservatism had been heavily penetrated by Objectivist college students, resulting in a gradually escalating conflict with the 'trads'. The sudden withdrawal of Rand's followers settled this conflict decisively. Although libertarian elements hung on in organizations such as Young Americans for Freedom for several years, without the impetus of Objectivism behind them they could make no progress and gradually diffused out. A threat to the traditional right's control of the conservative movement was thereby averted.

Rand no longer indulged in any political activity. She reluctantly and with many qualifications endorsed the presidential campaigns of Richard Nixon and Gerald Ford; she would not even do that much for Ronald Reagan. Ayn Rand had finally given up on conservatism. She had never accepted libertarianism. But—another Randian paradox—having retired from active political struggle, she wrote thereafter increasingly on political, rather than philosophical, subjects.

In examining this last period of Ayn Rand's life and thought, let us begin by examining American postwar conservatism and her reasons for rejecting it.

ROOTS OF THE NEW CONSERVATISM

The postwar intellectual renaissance of the Right contained three strands. Foremost, of course, was what is now called conservatism.

The conservatives of earlier eras—even the 1930s, let alone the nineteenth century—would scarcely have recognized modern conservatism. After the political disasters of the New Deal, conservatives revived their movement only by means of a quite thorough housecleaning. As a result, modern conservatism shares little with its predecessors beyond the classic emphasis on tradition and social stability, religion and morals. Many key principles of the old conservatism were abandoned or even reversed. Antisemitism was quietly repudiated, and racist notions of black inferiority and the 'yellow peril' were toned down to an occasional whisper. Protectionism was reluctantly abandoned. In the realm of foreign policy, the traditional isolationism was completely reversed with the adoption of a program of active intervention to oppose Communism.

The founders of the new conservatism smelted it from a

mixture of ideological ores which did not always fuse into a stable alloy. For a base they adopted—with reservations—the classical liberal critique of the State, in particular the argument of Friedrich Hayek's *The Road to Serfdom*. Long the defenders of strong central government, conservatives had finally learned during the New Deal what it was like to be at the wrong end of the big stick. To add intellectual tensile strength it was essential to mix in 'Austrian' economics with its advocacy of laissez-faire capitalism, repellant though this was to their traditional big-business constituency. The consistency of the melt was thickened with a fervent anti-Communism. Finally, to add luster and sheen to the surface, the Southern Agrarian tradition with its European aristocratic cachet was added.

With the resulting material, weakened though it was by its internal contradictions, conservatives felt strong enough to go on the offensive against the dominant liberal ideology. Yet for thirty years conservative political generals have managed to snatch defeat from the jaws of victory—just as Rand predicted all along. Scarcely an issue of *National Review* appears that does not bemoan the great problem of conservatives: they can't seem to actually make any changes in government, even when elections give them the 'power'. Conservative politicians somehow fail to implement their right-wing views. (For eight years conservatives muttered darkly about advisors who wouldn't 'let Reagan be Reagan'.) American foreign policy remains left-liberal in trend no matter who is President, and appeasement of communism and terrorism continues no matter whom he appoints as Secretary of State. Conservative Supreme Court nominees strangely become 'moderate' or even 'liberal' justices as soon as they take their seats.

RAND'S CRITIQUE OF CONSERVATISM

Rand's most trenchant and specific attack on conservatism was developed in her essay 'Conservatism, an Obituary'.[3] At this time (1960) she had already clearly identified the weakness of modern conservatism and foreseen its inevitable impotence to reverse or even halt the trend to statism. Though she took up this theme again in her articles during the Goldwater campaign, during the next decade Rand concentrated her fire on the liberals, most notably in her articles on the 'consensus' politics of Lyndon Johnson.

Rand, with her obsession with consistency, saw all along the defect in conservatism: its internal contradictions. Despite the ingenious efforts of Michael Novak and George Gilder, it is difficult to reconcile the Judeo-Christian morality of altruism with laissez-faire, a system based on self-interest. A reverence for tradition tends to conflict with the goal of imposing American cultural and political forms on other countries. The belief that it is the duty of the State to supervise the moral education, sexual behavior, and reading habits of the people is scarcely compatible with opposition to strong government. Since to be a 'principled' conservative is a logical impossibility—the principles of conservatism being mutually contradictory—any conservative who achieves political office will inevitably adapt himself to the expediency of the moment—which means grovelling to the special-interest groups.

The process by which such contradictions corrupt the political process was described by Rand in her *Objectivist Newsletter* article 'The Anatomy of a Compromise' (January, 1964). More than 20 years later, her predictions have been amply born out:

> It is precisely those ends (altruism-collectivism-statism) that ought to be rejected. But if neither party chooses to do it, the logic of events created by their common basic principles will keep dragging them both further and further to the left.[4]

With time the conservative movement has managed to absorb some ideas from—Ayn Rand. For example, during the 1980s 'entrepreneurship' came into vogue not only in business management, but in the political literature. The leader in this apotheosis of the business founder was George Gilder, a thinker who admits to having been influenced by Rand's writings. Gilder led the way in celebrating the importance of the entrepreneur in economic growth and increasing employment—ideas that are central to (though not original in) *Atlas Shrugged*. Gilder also makes much of the "essential altruism" of the entrepreneur, the fact that he creates far more than he is ever compensated for. This is a primitive distortion of Rand's insight that great innovators leave mankind a legacy so great that they can never be fully repaid.[5]

Having rejected conservatism, Rand might have been expected to embrace the younger political philosophy described by the rather awkward term 'libertarianism'. But she didn't.

THE EVOLUTION OF LIBERTARIANISM

Developing in parallel with, but more slowly than the conservative movement, there appeared what is now referred to as the libertarian movement. Again, much of the basis for this ideology was provided by the Austrian economists, especially through the mediation of Murray Rothbard. But the movement drew greatly on early individualist thinkers such as Lysander Spooner, Albert J. Nock, Frank Chodorov, and Rose Wilder Lane.

Although the conservative movement is scarcely monolithic, one can discuss American 'conservatism' with a reasonable notion of a specific set of ideas to which one is referring. The same cannot be said for libertarianism. Unlike modern conservatism, libertarianism makes not even a pretense of unity or consistency. Much of the movement consists of limited-government advocates who in essence agree with Ayn Rand's political position, though they are reluctant to mention her name. Represented by *Reason* magazine, they are sometimes derided by more radical anarchist types as 'coffee-table libertarians'. Then there are various flavors of anarchists, ranging from the 'vonuists' who try to eliminate their vulnerability to government oppression by hiding in the woods or joining a truly 'underground' economy by living in caves, to radical pacifists like Robert Lefevre. Drifting in and out of the movement are what might be called 'opportunistic libertarians'— people who have some specific beef with the government, but no real philosophical affinity for libertarian ideas.

THE ESSENCE OF LIBERTARIANISM

Can we find any unifying factor—any 'essence'—that will give us a useful definition of libertarianism (as distinct from classical liberalism)? If we can define libertarianism at all, we will do best to characterize it as a spectrum of political philosophies which regard the State as, inherently, an evil. Some libertarians may regard it as a necessary evil, or an unavoidable evil. But anyone who sees government as capable of being intrinsically good ought not to be considered a true libertarian. If we accept this concept of libertarianism, then we may say that in its purest or most radical form it must advocate the actual abolition of government. This in fact is what the line of thought usually referred to as 'anarcho-capitalism' aims at.[6]

It is important to get at the root of the anarcho-capitalist position, because it deals with the most fundamental question of political theory: the origin of the State. The radical libertarian critique of politics gives us a new perspective from which we can more clearly understand the problem which Objectivism must deal with.

As soon as political theory moved beyond primitive 'might makes right' or religious justifications of the State, the basic issue of politics was re-opened in new form. What is, or could be, the origin of the Just State? Why ought citizens to accept its authority?

ROOTS OF THE POLITICAL CONFLICT

Most commentators see the fundamental debate of the modern era as a continuing clash between the ideas of two political philosophers, Hobbes and Locke. Though the battle line is not always clear cut, this dichotomy remains the best means of understanding the issue.

For Hobbes, human beings are inherently vicious and, left to their own devices, will live without society in a war of all against all. As his most famous phrase puts it, man's life in a "state of nature" (that is, a state of freedom) will be "solitary, poor, nasty, brutish, and short". Fortunately, the State relieves mankind from this unpleasant condition by curbing and taming humanity's evil tendencies and enforcing society and co-operation. In this vision the State is inherently good and just; even if oppressive, the government does not make its subjects' lives as terrible as they would be if the State did not exist. In other words, anything is better than anarchy.

Locke takes a somewhat more optimistic view of human nature. People may not be perfect, but they have a great capacity for decency and are inclined to choose good rather than evil. Life in a 'state of nature' is less than optimal, but men can, and if given the chance will, form their own society and government in order to better their state. A government constituted in this way—and only such a government—is just, because it develops out of the voluntary choice of the people it governs.

In other words, the approach of Hobbes says that government is inherently good, and thus just, because it benefits the people. The approach of Locke says that government may or may not be good; it is just only when it is the choice of the people. Hobbes relies on an appeal to welfare; Locke on the concept of rights.

Hobbes never lost his hold on intellectuals in Europe, and the primary political tradition there is the primacy of the State. The default, so to speak, is with the government: It may be well to have some limits placed on the State (such as the Magna Carta), but in general the government may do anything that is not specifically prohibited to it. In the political arena of twentieth-century America, this position has been most commonly associated with what Americans call 'liberalism'. However, it has also had a strong attraction to conservatives. Indeed, perhaps the most eloquent American spokesman for the primacy of the State is the conservative jurist, Robert Bork.

Locke, however, took hold in revolutionary America. His political philosophy leads to giving the default to the people: The government may do nothing except to execute those functions specifically allowed to it by the people who created it.[7] This view was virtually universal among the Founders, whether Federalist or Anti-Federalist. However, support for it has gradually eroded, so that now only a small minority of Americans accept it. Only among Objectivists and libertarians does it receive consistent support.

What, then, do Objectivists and libertarians have to argue about? A naive observer might find it difficult to understand why these two groups should be at each other's throats. The writings of the two sides seldom address the real issues clearly, but on analysis we can see that both have a case to make.

Objectivism versus Libertarianism: The Case for the Plaintiff

Libertarianism, which even more than conservatism is an ideological melange, was scarcely likely to impress Ayn Rand as the vanguard of the future. Her dislike of the modern libertarian movement was at least as violent as her distaste for conservatism. It is likely that part of her opposition arose from the conspicuous position in the libertarian movement of Murray Rothbard, an apostate (in her view) from Objectivism. After the Great Schism, Nathaniel Branden became a prominent feature of the libertarian subculture, which no doubt exacerbated her feelings on the subject.

However, to ascribe Rand's opposition solely to personal factors is to underestimate her sadly. By the time this ideology appeared on the scene in its modern form, Ayn Rand was a very mature thinker with deep insight into the ethical roots of politics and a shrewd understanding of practical politics as well as ideology. The intellectual flowering of anarcho-capitalism in the 1970s produced more enthusiasm than practical thinking, and with her usual ability to put her finger on the key problems, Rand turned out to be right in essence if not in detail.

There are a number of practical objections which might be raised to anarcho-capitalist models, and Rand quickly zeroed in on the apparent absurdity of the idea of 'competing governments'. (The anarcho-capitalists would say 'competing defense agencies'.) What are the consequences, she asks, when agents of one government attempt to arrest a subscriber to a different, competing government?[8] On examination, this objection seems to lose force. How is the same problem handled now? For we have competing governments right now; they simply don't share the same geographical territory.[9] If, for instance, an American citizen is accused of a crime against a Canadian, the Canadian government asks for his extradition. Of course, a service business might be reluctant to extradite one of its customers! But after all, a national government is generally reluctant to extradite a citizen, and the political imperatives can be just as strong as economic motives. The extradition problem is not a serious objection from a practical point of view. However, in raising it Rand hints at her real reason for opposing competing governments: If governments are just, they cannot differ.

A more substantive objection, much debated within the libertarian movement, is the 'free rider' problem. A government's services, particularly defense against foreign aggressors, are hard to individuate. A 'defense agency' that protects one subscriber in, say, Seattle from nuclear attack can hardly do so without protecting the whole city. Most inhabitants of the area are likely to refrain from subscribing to such a costly service, since they will get the benefit for free anyway. They are 'free riders'.

But in Rand's analysis, the radical libertarians fail on epistemological grounds. The anarcho-capitalist position is a politics based on subjectivism. In essence, their argument is, 'There's no objective basis for controlling the use of force. Your belief that you're using force to protect yourself is just an opinion; what if it is my opinion that you are violating my rights?' Thus the anarchocapitalist invokes 'the market' as a sort of mystical, godlike force that will somehow, automatically, solve the problem of justice in a way that is beyond the capabilities of individual human beings.[10]

The Objectivist argument against libertarianism has been summed up in an essay by Peter Schwartz.[11] "Libertarianism," he says, "is a version of moral subjectivism." It is a political ideology with no moral or philosophical grounding; this is shown by the widely varying, and violently contradictory, moral theories of its adherents. When Murray Rothbard, Robert Poole Jr., Walter Block, and Milton Friedman are all accepted as libertarians, the ideology must be considered eclectic, to say the least. But if there is no moral basis for politics, then how is one to understand political conflicts? Only by introducing a libertarian version of 'class warfare', in which those who benefit from the State oppress those who pay for their benefits. So the logical conclusion, says Schwartz, quoting some 'radical' libertarians, is violence. If ideas are not the source of ideology, then 'education' is useless, and only a resort to armed force can overcome the State.

Schwartz has a field day depicting libertarians as monsters, adducing 'horror file' quotes from thinkers across much of the libertarian spectrum to support his points. He anticipates the protests of those libertarians who *don't* believe that the U.S. is the world's foremost oppressor or that pederasty should be legalized. Libertarianism, Schwartz points out, must be thought of in terms of its essential characteristics. And by his definition, the essence of libertarianism is nihilism.

Certainly the critique of libertarianism developed by Rand and elaborated by Schwartz has a great deal of force. It is perceptive, and fundamentally correct, in stating that the key problem with libertarianism is its aversion to grounding political principles in moral philosophy. The detachment of politics from ethics, the attempt to make politics as *wertfrei* (value-free) as Austrian economics, is doomed to failure—and dooms its adherents to failure.

However: While agreeing that the hierarchical structure of knowledge requires that political philosophy be based on ethics, I cannot accompany Schwartz the rest of the way. In his eagerness to condemn the people, he has incorrectly defined the idea. Moral subjectivism is certainly a characteristic of most libertarian thought—but it is not the essence. In epistemological terms, it is merely an 'accidental' characteristic. The true essence of libertarianism is, as I have said above, that it challenges the idea that government can be a good in itself. This idea may be wrong—but it is not nihilism. Anarcho-capitalists say that, in some way, market forces can produce justice better than a government can, just as they can produce shoes better than a collective can. This is not the same thing as saying that there is no such thing as justice, or that justice is undesirable.

OBJECTIVISM VERSUS LIBERTARIANISM: THE CASE FOR THE DEFENDANT

The anarchist stream within the libertarian movement has its own case to make, and it is a cogent one. The root of the anarcho-libertarian argument is, in effect, a critique of the concept of the 'social contract'.[12]

As we have seen, the American political tradition derives from the natural rights theory of Locke and states that "to secure these rights, governments are instituted among men, deriving their just powers from the consent of the governed." To this the anarcho-libertarian replies, 'Wait a minute! When did *I* consent? Show me this social contract—where's my signature?'

For the social contract is not really a contract, since it is imposed by force. The terms are dictated, not freely chosen. Of course, they may be reasonable terms. 'It takes money to pay for policemen and courts and an army to protect you; if you want to be a citizen you must pay taxes, or some equivalent, to fund these services.' But in practice the terms tend to become somewhat less reasonable. 'We have to have an army to deal with foreign aggression, and no amount of money will hire enough soldiers, or the right kind. So if you want to be a citizen, you must accept being drafted.'

The strong point of the anarcho-capitalist critique is that Locke's compact between government (or 'society') and citizen is not really voluntary. The State makes, in the Godfather's famous phrase, an offer one cannot refuse. The individual must sign or, at minimum, be forcibly ejected from the country of his birth. (This was the choice faced in very practical terms by Tories during the American Revolution.) So Locke's Just State is nothing of the kind, for its basic moral justification—voluntary acceptance by its citizens—does not really exist.

The anarcho-capitalists therefore reject the social contract as a group contract. They demand an arrangement under which each person can voluntarily make an individual social contract. But if government is a monopoly, those who reject its terms have no viable options, so that the 'consent of the governed' is extorted, not truly voluntary. So government must be a function of the market, just like any other service, with competing 'defense agencies' providing police, military, and judicial services.

In this interpretation, the anarcho-capitalist position must be conceded to have great force. Of course many practical objections (such as the 'free rider' argument mentioned above) have been raised. However, let us bypass issues of this sort and stick with the key issue: What is the origin of the Just State?

OBJECTIVISM AND THE THEORY OF GOVERNMENT

Having examined Rand's interpretation, and critique, of conservatism and libertarianism, we are now entitled to ask what positive vision she offers. What is her own theory of politics, and what does she offer as a model of the Just State?

Rand's 'limited government' is consistent with her approach to epistemology. Justice is objective and knowable. Man can, by logical analysis, determine what justice is and construct a government which will enforce it. What is missing—and it is a crucial omission—in the Objectivist politics is a positive theory of the origin of government. What is government? What justifies it? Why should rational men submit to it? How does it, or should it, originate?

Let us examine Rand's closest approach to this fundamental problem, in her essay 'The Nature of Government'.[8] This basic paper on the Objectivist politics begins with an approach copied from the Objectivist ethics: Define the topic—and ask why it should exist at all.

> A government is an institution that holds the exclusive power to enforce certain rules of social conduct in a given geographical area.
>   Do men need such an institution—and why?

Rand goes on from this beginning to summarize her theory of rights (which is essentially plain vanilla natural rights theory, though based on Objectivist ethics). But she soon moves on from this topic to the question of the need for government. Her argument is that retaliatory use of force is necessary to prevent the individual from being left at the mercy of thugs. Anarchy is unacceptable:

> The use of physical force—even its retaliatory use—cannot be left at the discretion of individual citizens.

It is therefore necessary to develop objective laws, objective rules of evidence, and an institution charged with implementing and enforcing those laws. Government places "the retaliatory use of force under objective control."

So far we may follow Rand without difficulty. But now comes the hard part. Though she quotes with approval the American principle that the source of government authority is "the consent of the governed", Rand fails to consider how that consent is to be obtained. If she rejects the anarcho-libertarian approach—that the individual may freely choose whether to give the consent to be governed—what alternative does she propose? What is the source or origin of government? Rand simply dodges this issue. She says 'society' is to provide organized protection against force. Doesn't sound much like Ayn Rand's usual mode of thought, does it? Where is the Ayn Rand we are used to—the one who would ask, 'Just who is this "society" and how is it decided what "geographical area" the government may properly police?' 'Society' as used here is just the sort of floating abstraction that Rand so vigorously attacked in her other work.

Having bravely stepped into this intellectual quagmire, Rand found herself sinking deeper when she took up the issue of government financing. Her essay, 'Government Financing in a Free Society'[13] begins to flounder in the first few paragraphs. Sounding perilously similar to the socialists who tell us that problems with their system will be solved 'somehow', Rand says that the question of government financing is a "very complex one" and that getting down to specifics is premature. She immediately concedes that taxation is an initiation of force and therefore impermissible. But, though avoiding this sinkhole, she is unable to find a path through the morass.

Tentatively she suggests a possible solution: a stamp tax. Of course she does not call it that; it is characterized as a fee for the service of enforcing contracts. And in fact this fund-raising mechanism, which is also advocated by many libertarians, would not be a 'tax'—except that Rand states that "only a government" can enforce contracts. In reality—even in the present-day U.S.— most contracts depend on non-legal sanctions. With rare exceptions, both industrial and consumer agreements are enforced not by threat of lawsuit but by threat of refusing to carry out or renew transactions. In the cases where this informal sanction fails, private arbitrators and other mechanisms are taking a growing amount of "business" away from the government courts. How would Rand's government deal with this private competition?

Rand's other suggestion—a government lottery—runs into the same problem. Would she outlaw private gambling? If not, how will a socialized lottery compete in the market? The difficulty is general. Any proposal that the State 'earn its keep' must face the historical fact that governments are not good at running businesses.

What about other government services? Exactly how could

one charge the users of police services, let alone military services? Rand raises the question only to dodge it. Developing an answer, she says, "has to be regarded as a goal for a distant future". (Like Engels's withering away of the State, no doubt.) Instead, she finishes the essay with a re-hash of her critique of existing governments and their taxing and spending habits.

Rand's evident problems with the government financing question arise from the fact that it involves the literal implementation of the 'social contract'. To specify exactly how citizens will be charged for government services, one must first consider the terms of their contract with the government and how they were reached. This is precisely the question that Rand failed to resolve.

Rand's View of Man and Society

As we have seen, Objectivist political theory is vulnerable to the anarcho-libertarian critique because Rand's work in this area failed to delve to the roots of the subject and deal with the inherent weakness of Locke's concept of government. She has, so to speak, built her house on the sand. But cannot the situation be retrieved? Let us ask how we might proceed if we wish to build a positive theory to justify Rand's 'limited government' position.

There are strong implications, especially in Rand's fiction, that she was groping toward what might be called a 'super-Lockean' approach—or, more precisely, a return to Aristotle.

Aristotle's famous assertion that "Man is a political animal" is in fact a mistranslation. Converting it literally from the Greek gives, "Man is an animal whose nature it is to live in a *polis* [a city-state]." For Aristotle, man is naturally social, and it is his nature and good for him to live in society, just as it is the nature of antelope to live in herds or monkeys to live in trees.

Modern political philosophy is based on a radically different view of man. It begins with Hobbes and Locke, though Hume, Rousseau, Mill, and many others have contributed to it. Throughout their many vigorous disagreements, political theorists of the modern tradition have united in their belief that there is a fundamental conflict between the good of the individual and his entry into society. Men's interests, in this view, are naturally in conflict; the function of society is to suppress this conflict, by forcibly repressing the self-interest of the individual. Locke was perhaps the least pessimistic of these philosophers. His view was that an intelligent, rational man could perceive that it was in his long-run self-interest to join society. Although, even for Locke, men's interests are inherently in conflict, the individual will gain from his co-operation with other men more than he loses by renouncing the chance to attack them, thus developing a net profit from his socialization.

Where would Rand fit into this debate? Since politics is a corollary of ethics, we find Rand constrained very tightly by her ethical egoism. This compels her to take the position that there is no conflict of interests among rational men.

The classical philosophical 'refutation' of ethical egoism is an attempt to reduce it to absurdity as follows: 'Suppose the egoist wants some particular thing—say, to marry a certain woman. How would he counsel another man who would benefit by marrying the same woman? If he tells him to court her, the egoist is going against his own self-interest; if he tells him not to court her, he is advising the other man not to be an egoist. Thus egoism contains an inherent contradiction.'

Rand bulls her way through this problem by simply cutting the Gordian knot: She asserts that there is not, and cannot be, any conflict of interests among rational men. Thus she makes a point of challenging this argument explicitly in *Atlas Shrugged* by embodying precisely the example given in the competition between Rearden, Francisco, and John Galt for the favors of Dagny Taggart.

Rand repudiates the basic idea of modern political theory, for she does not believe that seeking values by force is practical or 'selfish'. Thus she goes Locke one better; man's entry into society is, or at least ought to be, pure profit. In giving up the chance to live as a predator, the individual is losing nothing. It is not commonly appreciated that this is one of Rand's most radical positions. In a typically Randian paradox, this quintessential individualist counters the philosophical tradition that men are naturally individuals.

As we saw in Chapter 5, a key theme in *Atlas Shrugged*—derived directly from Aristotle—is the idea that man is naturally social. Statist government creates not society, but a perversion of society, which drives the best men into isolation and cuts them off from human intercourse. What Rand saw as an ideal society, her "utopia of greed" in Galt's Gulch, is one in which government is so unobtrusive as to be almost invisible. Her heroes have no laws, only customs and an arbitrator to settle any disagreements—of which there are none. Rational men, living together, have no conflicts. It is ironic indeed that the one example of ideal government which Rand shows us is a culture of unmitigated anarchy.

Unfortunately, this approach to politics is, in a very literal sense, utopian: Its implementation would require a society made up exclusively of rational men. The logic of Rand's position forces her to focus on morality, for a moral citizenry is a prerequisite for her political system. The modern political tradition aims at a social structure which will, at minimum, function with an imperfect citizenry, and preferably result in their moral improvement. Rand does not regard this as possible; morality produces good government, not the other way around.

In this she is at one with America's founders who, following Montesquieu and a tradition going back to ancient Rome and further, believed no republic could operate successfully unless its citizens valued rectitude above all. As an inscription in Oregon's State Capitol puts it:

> In the souls of its citizens will be found the likeness of the State; which, if they be unjust and tyrannical, then will it reflect their vices; but if they be lovers of righteousness, confident in their liberties, so will it be clean in justice, bold in freedom.[14]

In the end Rand's position is that morality provides not only the intellectual but the practical foundation of politics. No political theory can be sound unless it is thoroughly grounded on the basis of the Objectivist ethics. And, it would seem, no just government can survive unless the citizens exhibit Objectivist virtues.

The problems with the foundation of Objectivist politics remain unsolved. We cannot find an adequate justification for Rand's position. However, at least we have clearly delineated where it fits into the debate. To provide a simplified summary: Hobbes justifies the State on the basis of its benefit to the people.

Locke regards the State as just provided it reflects the choice of the people. Rand's Objectivist Just State is to merit its authority because it implements objective, knowable moral principles. For the anarcho-libertarians, the State by definition is imposed without the consent of the individual, and so nothing can justify government.

Libertarians not unnaturally are wary of accepting the principle that government can be justified because it enforces morality. History provides too many examples of the abuse of this justification—from the theocracies of old to modern totalitarian states. Yet they need a stronger counter-argument than moral subjectivism. For what is the argument from the 'consent of the governed' if not a moral argument? When they assert that neither Objectivism nor any other morality can be logically justified, they cut the ground from under their own feet. The desire for *wertfrei Freiheit* is ultimately a contradiction in terms.

THE FINAL DECLINE

Rand's difficulties with the theory of government exemplify the decline of her powers during this concluding, 'political period' of her career. Her last writings, the essays she published in *The Ayn Rand Letter*, are her weakest. During the 1970s, while she was writing this material, Rand suffered from lung cancer. The effects of ill-health are evident in the frequent publication delays and, unfortunately, in the content of the articles. Rand's analysis is, in these essays, frequently superficial and crude. The rapier is replaced by the bludgeon, the fierce crusader now strikes her blows with a weary arm.

Much of the weakness of Rand's last series of essays results from her frequent choice of rather trivial subject matter. The writer who once dealt with the rise and fall of philosophies and civilizations was now analyzing *New York Times* editorials and discussing the significance of Boris Spassky. *The Ayn Rand Letter* might better have been titled *John Galt's Breakfast*.

Still, almost to the end Rand was producing useful insights. Her critique of Rawl's *A Theory of Justice* is incisive, though not up to her best work. In another essay on the fall of Vietnam, her comparison to the Russian Civil War is perceptive and illuminating.

At the end, Rand's last article in *The Ayn Rand Letter* sounds tired and disillusioned. She seems to feel that her work has had little influence on American and world politics, though she cites some possible counter-examples. Her tone, if not her words, is pessimistic. One may ascribe this simply to the fact of her age and illness. Or, perhaps one should credit her remarkable intuition; this last letter was written on the eve of the Carter era. Caught between the Scylla of Carter and the Charybdis of Reagan, Rand could favor neither. Nor could she throw her support to the nascent libertarian movement. With NBI destroyed, the Collective mostly excommunicated, and the Objectivist movement reduced to a minuscule, inbred clique, where could she see any hope? Only by reverting to her emphasis on the realm of the intellect, the importance of philosophy.

The final essay in her posthumous book, *Philosophy: Who Needs It*, is titled, 'Don't Let It Go', echoing Eddie Willers's cry as he futilely attempts to re-start the last of the Taggart engines. It is a cry of despair.

So, whither Objectivist politics? Where do we go from here?

THE PATH LESS TRAVELLED

The libertarian movement, following the line initiated by Rand's article 'It's Earlier Than You Think' has adopted the 'educationist' approach. If only we can convince the population, spread the correct ideas, they will vote for the right candidates and changes will be made. But, as we have seen in the 1980s, any changes which result will be superficial and ephemeral. One recalls Hank Rearden's belief, after the John Galt Line triumph, that "all that stuff will be swept away". As Rand had recognized as early as the 1950s, politics doesn't work that way.

As we have seen, Rand's political thought converged with the basic principle of the American Founders (and not original with them) that good government flows from the virtue of the citizens. Good leaders are available in any generation—but will they be elected? A shrewdly designed constitution may be written—but will it be obeyed? The electorate may be educated in economics and political philosophy—but will that induce them to vote against their own subsidies? For Rand, as for those who founded this country, it is clear that practical political results flow from moral choices.

Libertarians have never lost the obsession, rooted in Austrian economics, with 'value-neutral' or *wertfrei* political theory. They have revolted against Rand's unification of 'ought' and 'is', rejected her insistence on making politics the handmaiden of morality. Instead, they have sought to 'broaden' their support by appealing to the 'New Left' and other discontented portions of society. The most obvious feature of libertarian political propaganda has been the appeal to moral tolerance: Vote for us, and you can smoke marijuana, live in a commune without being hassled, or work as a prostitute. This approach has not proved successful in arousing fervent enthusiasm in large numbers of people.

Rand's insight remains valid: Political success is more likely to result from taking the moral high ground, even if only small forces occupy it, than from leading a large mob into the swamp. For, in the area of political strategy, Rand leads us in a direction diametrically opposed to modern libertarian theory. As we discussed above, the essence of the libertarian approach is to entice supporters by offering tolerance. This seems quite logical; what we are offering, after all, is the removal of government restrictions. How can we expect potential allies to join us in the fight for freedom if we condemn them as evil or immoral? How can we have political tolerance without moral tolerance?

Ayn Rand saw it differently. Political freedom, she asserts, can exist only in an atmosphere of rigid moral intolerance.[15] If we are to implement Rand's approach to government, we must return to her key idea of "the sanction of the victim". Her insight was really very simple: statists are, in essence, bullies. Whether they are Nazi Brownshirts breaking up an opposition rally, 'New Left' activists shouting down Edward Teller at a physics lecture, or environmentalists disrupting a corporate stockholders' meeting, the psychology is the same. They are, like schoolyard bullies, cowards at heart. Present them with firm and principled opposition, and their facade of confidence breaks up.

As Rand knew from her early experiences under Communism,

the thugs thrive on tolerance. Like dogs, they watch a potential victim intently, seeking even the slightest sign of uncertainty, the slightest hint of willingness to compromise—and if they find it, they attack. So, she concluded, the only solution was a complete withdrawal of moral sanction. One must give one's opposition nothing; one must offer no compromise; one must allow no tolerance.

Withdrawing the sanction of the victim is at the heart of Rand's political strategy. The actual strike which she presented in *Atlas Shrugged* is merely one variation on this theme. For Ayn Rand the only solution to government oppression—whether for the individual or for society—is the withdrawal of moral sanction. In this view, libertarians are, at best, scabs.

Rand's insight is compelling—but not without its dangers. Moral intolerance carries, as a tactical implication, the hazard of infighting and schism. This drawback must be dealt with if the Objectivist political program—or, indeed, Objectivism itself—is to have a future.

8 | THE FUTURE
OF OBJECTIVISM

Does Objectivism have a future?
Yes—but not, perhaps, along the lines that have commonly been envisioned.

A SECOND CRUSADE?

The dream of reviving the exciting days of NBI—the vision of Objectivism as an intellectual and moral crusade—still beckons. What of Objectivism as a unified movement?

Rand's own thinking on this question evolved during her lifetime. At first she did not envision an organized movement at all. She saw Objectivism as gradually becoming predominant in the field of philosophy and spreading through the intellectual structure of civilization—like any other idea, only better. She seems to have hoped that Objectivist philosophy would take over from what she perceived as the dominant Kantian philosophy; but at that time she probably would not have thought of an Objectivist 'movement' any more than she would have recognized a Kantian 'movement'.

With the success of NBI—a success she had not thought possible—her thinking began to change. In spite of her skepticism, a movement did indeed form. Objectivism became more than a set of ideas. Nathaniel and Barbara Branden developed an organization with a mission, assembling a group of like-minded people, and serving a social as well as an ideological function. Rand realized—and she seems to have found it rather disconcerting—that her ideas were now unifying a significant social force of young people. She felt compelled to take the lead.

In the process, her ideas of intellectual progress were modified. Up until the early 1960s, Rand seems to have accepted the process by which her ideas were incorporated piecemeal by other thinkers. Though another intellectual might not be consistent in his agreement with Objectivism, if he took some of it his thinking would at least be better; the next generation could take even more, and eventually the contradictions would be eliminated and Objectivism as a fully consistent philosophy would be accepted.

But as she became involved with NBI and *The Objectivist*, Rand's attitude changed. Now Objectivism was a movement. And as an organized movement, it had new imperatives. Rand, as always, was consistent. Once she accepted the desirability of an Objectivist movement, she did not hesitate to go all the way with the implications thereof. A movement must know who is part of it and who is not. There must be a party line. There must be a mechanism to prevent corruption of the party line. There must be enforcement procedures to prevent schisms, by crushing dissent before it can become strong enough to threaten the unity of the movement. Rand understood all this, and did not shrink from it.

Her followers, for the most part, did not understand it. Many accepted the new policy blindly. Others—including Nathaniel and Barbara Branden—became somewhat disillusioned with Rand. The doctrinaire approach, the 'excommunications', the viciously insulting statement, "Our job is to tell people *what* Objectivism is; your job is to tell them *that* it is."—all these were discomforting to many of us. Rand seemed to have adopted the manner of a power-luster. But this evaluation wrongs her at least partially. Rand simply understood, what those around her did not, that such procedures were necessary once the decision had been taken to develop an organized movement. That initial decision may have been wrong; and Rand's implementation of her enforcement procedures was crude, inefficient, and often cruel. But some such methods must be used by anyone who wishes to continue an organized 'Objectivist movement'—and they are.[1]

Rand's policies were also influenced by her concept of "the sanction of the victim" and her commitment to systematic moral intolerance. She understood that it was not easy to be an Objectivist, especially in an irrational society. As we have seen, Rand accepted from Nietzsche the idea that personal moral and intellectual growth is often painful, and that helping someone to grow means in a sense to be cruel to him. Finally, she knew from experience that no one can achieve rationality without a commitment to unbreached consistency, and so she came to believe that those who only partly agreed with her would be, in the end, worse than useless. She saw the NBI structure, one suspects, as a support system for young converts, a set of training wheels to keep them from falling away from Objectivist principles until they were competent to maintain integrity by themselves.

The problem which arises, though, is that a movement requires leadership—not only intellectual leadership but managerial leadership, and indeed in a broad sense political leadership. Someone must not only develop and police the ideas but develop and police the people. Rand was only fairly well suited to performing the first function, and not suited at all to performing the second. Still, her leadership was accepted because of her evident genius. People—even very intelligent people—tolerated being insulted, intimidated, and bullied by Ayn Rand. They do not seem so willing to tolerate it from her successors.

In the end it appears that an "Objectivist movement" was not, and is not, a very good idea. The rump movement which has survived Rand's death appears increasingly irrelevant to the progress of her ideas.

OR THE IVORY TOWER?

If we are not to promote the success of Objectivism by setting up an organization of 'intellectual activists', perhaps we should follow the approach suggested by Rand's analysis in her essay 'For the New Intellectual'. Let us develop a new generation of Hugh Akstons who will conquer the philosophy departments of academia; then Objectivist thinking will trickle down to the masses.

Rand, as noted before, disdained to present her philosophy in the standard academic forums. But she developed a few disciples, notably Leonard Peikoff and Harry Binswanger, who have attempted to carry Objectivist ideas into the ivory tower of the professional philosophers. Others, including Tibor Machan, John Hospers, and David Kelley, have joined in the work. There now exists an Ayn Rand Society within the American Philosophical Association. Even so, it appears that they are talking primarily to each other (and often not even that!); they don't seem to have made any impression on other philosophers.

A few noted modern philosophers have taken Rand, or at least some of her ideas, fairly seriously. Robert Nozick analyzed 'The Randian Argument' in a well-known article. And lately there has been an apparent revival of Aristotelian philosophies in general. Mortimer Adler's *Ten Philosophical Mistakes* reasserts the Aristotelian position on major issues in philosophy. Henry B. Veatch recently published *Human Rights: Fact or Fancy?*, which defends natural rights theory from an Aristotelian ethical basis. But again, these are mere islets in the tide of philosophical relativism. The tide may have turned; but if it is ebbing at all, it is receding only slowly.

It seems likely that Objectivism will have minimal influence on academic philosophy for the foreseeable future. It is not so much that academic philosophers are hostile to Objectivist ideas (though they very definitely are) as that they just don't think in that way. Objectivism did not grow out of the academic mainstream, even as a revolt against it; if it had, it might have been better received. Rather, Objectivism is totally alien, an outsider; it is nearly incomprehensible to the current philosophic mainstream in its focus, its approach, and even its terminology. Above all, academia finds Objectivism totally indigestible because of the philosophy's inherent and aggressive anti-relativism.

Will the day ever come when Objectivism gets a place in the philosophy curriculum? That will be the day!—when Ayn Rand is taken as seriously as Plato or Kant or Mill—when textbooks devote a chapter or so to her ideas—when students learn about Objectivism and carefully compare and contrast its tenets to those of other schools of thought. That will be the day when professors will no longer fear Objectivism—because it will be dead.

If we truly accept what Objectivism teaches, we must aim for a goal consistent with its premisses. If we truly believe that reality *is,* and is *knowable,* then we can ultimately accept nothing less than that philosophy should be treated as a science—which means: the total rejection of relativism.

Can we achieve this? Can we foresee an environment in which the university philosophy curriculum gives as much time to Plato's Cave as the chemistry curriculum does to the Philosopher's Stone? In which a philosopher who accepts Kant's metaphysics will be no more employable than a mathematician who believes he can square the circle? In which those who deny the possibility of a rational ethics will be taken as seriously as Flat Earth enthusiasts? For if we are really Objectivists, we must know that Objectivism is not just one of many contending schools of thought; it is— the truth.

I do not see much prospect that Objectivism will overcome the academic world's passionate commitment to philosophical relativism. Indeed, I have the impression that many even of Objectivism's scarce professorial defenders feel a certain ambivalence on the issue of relativism. It is safer, on campus, to advocate Naziism, or even the abolition of tenure, than to assert that one's philosophical opponents are objectively wrong, out of court, and that their positions are not credible enough to be taught.

Professional philosophers of an Objectivist bent will no doubt continue their efforts, and it is well that they should. But let us realistically recognize that they face a redoubt which, in spite of the ivy that covers it, is very formidable indeed. We can but salute the forlorn hope as they march off to their suicide mission. Fortunately, the front on which they are fighting is not the only strategic point, nor even the main one.

THE SCHOOLROOM OR THE POLLING BOOTH

Perhaps a more broad-based education approach would do better. Can we enlighten opinion leaders or even the 'masses' directly? Or perhaps even get into practical politics? This has been the strategy adopted by libertarians. How well has it worked?

We can say at once that the Libertarian Party shows no prospects of revolutionizing American politics. It has yet to demonstrate a growth trend by vote counts or any other measure. Having fought to date five presidential election campaigns, it can no longer justify failure on the grounds of inexperience or immaturity.

But what of other advances? Are not libertarian ideas and libertarian policies making progress? The twentieth anniversary issue of *Reason* magazine[2] offered a litany of celebration. Owning gold is now legal, lawyers can advertise, and an unmarried couple can share a hotel room without signing the register 'Mr. and Mrs.' And, to be fair, the last 20 years have seen some major advances for the cause of freedom in the United States: partial deregulation of the transportation and communication industries; tax reform, with a big drop in the nominal top rate; the end of military conscription.[3]

Nonetheless, an objective observer would have to conclude that American freedoms have, overall, declined precipitously in the last two decades. Government agencies have grown like weeds at every level, and businesses now face a regulatory environment that makes Directive 10-289 look downright sensible. The Bill of Rights is under assault on a broad front, and judicial protections dating back to Colonial times—such as the presumption of innocence for those accused of crimes—have already been abridged. Political institutions have broken down, and many elections—especially those for House seats—have become mere formalities.

But has there not been a resurgence of libertarian ideas? Indeed there has. But it has shot its bolt. Twenty years ago we fought Keynesian ideas from the 1930s with Misesian ideas from the 1950s. Today it is we who are out of date. Even public-choice theory, the most exciting recent development, is to a great extent merely old wine in new mathematical bottles. The important current work in political science and economics involves application of new methodologies such as catastrophe theory, the mathematics of chaos, and strategy simulation. As these powerful new weapons are forged, defenders of the free market congratulate themselves on the superb arsenal with which they are now prepared to fight the last war.

As this is written, Communism is in disarray worldwide and, in the estimation of many, dying—though I, for one, will not feel comfortable till I see it buried at a crossroads with a stake through its heart. But we face a formidable challenge from newer and much more sophisticated statist ideologies such as environmentalism and feminism. So far libertarian writers have countered these rising trends with the same force and skill with which Republicans fought the welfare state. 'Me too—but can't we make do without such oppressive regulations?' is the plaintive cry.

Objectivist and libertarian intellectuals alike have become entirely too complacent. Very few are pushing ahead with novel ideas; instead, most continue to produce the same dreary critiques on yesterday's issues. Rather than courageous criticism of the FAA or farm subsidies or auto import quotas, we need work on fundamental questions. What positive vision of the future do we have to offer? Too often Objectivists, as well as libertarians, seem to offer the past: turn the clock back to something approximating 1870 and keep it there. It is not going to happen, nor should it. Technology has changed, the economy has changed, society has changed—and our vision of the organization of the free society must change too.

There was a time when capitalism was *new*, when representative government was *new*. The future will hold undreamed-of ways of organizing society. They will be as unfamiliar to us as laissez faire was to the Mercantilists. The society of the future cannot simply evolve, though; it must be invented. That is our job. When are we going to get to work?

BACK TO THE FUTURE

If Objectivism is to have a future, we must return to the insights Ayn Rand gave us 30 years ago. The ultimate objective is not political, nor even intellectual, but cultural change. Ayn Rand teaches us that government is not a primary. We cannot succeed as long as we think of political reform as our primary task. Society is a three-legged stool which rests on its political system, its economic system, and its social values and organization. All three components must be in harmony. This goal is at once our greatest challenge, our greatest opportunity, and our greatest danger.

We must develop a vision, not just of a free economy, but of a free society. What are we really aiming at? The sort of nihilism so characteristic of modern ideologies, including much of libertarianism, aims at abolition of the society we have, but offers in return nothing but a vague image of a world in which 'everybody can do his own thing'. There is no such thing. Every society constrains its members in some way—free societies, by custom; the others by law.

And here is the irony, a final, posthumous Randian paradox: libertarianism has failed by its success. For libertarian ideas *have* triumphed to a great extent—not in the political, but in the social sphere. The moral consensus and corresponding social customs that once restricted Americans' behavior have been demolished. And this has been a major driving force for reduction of freedom in the political sphere. Today teenage girls can bear illegitimate babies without the terrible stigma that once attached to it. Now whole cities are filled with fatherless children and the welfare state grows to support them. Taking drugs became a matter of personal choice, not subject to moral censure. Now the public supports a police state to get rid of the crack dealers. Citizens demand—and it is not an irrational demand— that society be orderly, safe, and humane. Remove the 'oppression' of custom and morality, and you get the far worse oppression of government. The principles of social tolerance and moral relativism that Rand saw as the root evils of libertarianism have triumphed. Now the defenders of the indefensible face the political backlash. A voice from the grave says, "Brother, you asked for it!"[4]

Ayn Rand offers us a vision, incomplete though it is, of a society oriented to achievement. In her "Utopia of Greed", law is imperceptible; but the invisible hand of custom guides every member of society in the same direction. Whoever has a purpose to achieve—whether building a railroad, writing a concerto, or raising a child—is not only utterly free, but honored and supported. It is a free society—but not a tolerant one. In it the purposeless, the idle, the self-destructive have no place. They need not be criminals—but they will be outcasts. Here is a society both unfettered and orderly, a society with rules but no rulers, reigned over by an aristocracy of character which yet is open to anyone who chooses to enter it.

The task of Objectivism is to clarify, to elaborate, to fully understand this vision of society—and then to build it.

WHAT IS TO BE DONE?

The ultimate triumph of Objectivism depends on the process by which individuals absorb the philosophy into their lives. There is no royal road to Galt's Gulch, and society will not be re-formed by teachers or treatises. Objectivists can accomplish more by example than by instruction.

The full strategy and tactics of the coming struggle comprise a book which is yet to be written. Ayn Rand, in her life's work, barely started on the problem. We have only a few insights to give us a starting point.

To begin with, Objectivist intellectuals need to regain their self-confidence and their courage. They have too often become timid, stodgy, and conservative. Where today do we find the boldness, the radical originality, and the sheer zest that were so characteristic of Ayn Rand? Half of the genius of Ayn Rand was that she saw what everybody saw, and said what nobody dared to say. We need once again to become intellectual leaders, to have the courage to approach the cutting edge of new thought. If this means submerging our longing for acceptance and 'respectability', so be it.

The present situation of Objectivists is grotesque. Some of us huddle around the remnants of the old movement, tending the dying flame of Rand's writings but fearing to leave the firelit circle to find more fuel. Others go out into the world, but truly, indeed, do we hide our light under a bushel—ashamed to admit to our commitment or pronounce the forbidden name of Ayn Rand. There are those who cling to Rand—and renounce her principles of independent thought and radical innovation. There are those who cling to Objectivism—and are ashamed to mention its discoverer or speak up forcefully to defend their own beliefs.

Objectivists surely would accomplish more if they could agree to disagree on peripheral issues. Far from rebuilding and extending a culture of rationality, those who owe allegiance to Objectivism all too often repulse all attempts at reconciliation. Those who treat altruists, collectivists, and mystics with impeccable personal courtesy sneer and spit at rational men with whom they have no substantive disagreement. And—I speak now to both sides—do not open your mouth to tell me that the childish squabblings of the Great Schism constitute a substantive disagreement. Objectivists need to concentrate their attention on questions more fundamental than who slept with whom 30 years ago. Perhaps we should attend to the example of a man who, involved in a literally life-and-death struggle, could live with, and even love, the woman who had sworn to kill him.

LIFE SUPPORT SYSTEMS

The most serious damage inflicted by the Great Schism and the destruction of the NBI organization was the abortion of the embryo of an Objectivist culture. The NBI lectures, and the clubs and discussion groups which grew out of them, brought isolated Objectivists together. The movement began to become not just an arena for learning and debate, but a social meeting ground. We started to learn how to interact with other people in a new way; we took the first steps toward building a rational society. Then it was all destroyed.

Each of us who accepts Objectivism faces exactly the same problem that tormented Rand throughout her life: How can a rational person live in an irrational society? How can a sane man live in an insane culture? We too readily forget Rand's insight that we cannot truly do so alone.

We have learned from Rand the first step only—how to live with ourselves. But we are on our own from there, for she left us only a few hints.

How do we live with the irrational? Rand taught us the need for independence, for consistency, for loyalty to our values in spite of all pressures. And she taught us the danger of emotional repression. Yet, as we find ourselves in an increasingly regulated, statist, and hazardous world, we encounter the need for new ways of coping. Nathaniel Branden has contributed much useful work on this problem; more is needed.

How do we live with the rational? Rand gives us only a hint, with her brief vision of Galt's Gulch. Yet, in the long run, this is the most crucial question for the future of Objectivism. A society of rational persons will of necessity develop an entirely new set of social institutions. The organization not just of government, but of the economy, of education, of the family, and every other aspect of social life will be changed. It is none too soon to be thinking about these issues.

And, if Objectivism is to begin moving again, we must re-establish an Objectivist subculture. The influence of Objectivists as isolated individuals is too limited. More important, to maintain Objectivist ideals as a lone and lonely individual is too stressful. We would be immensely strengthened—politically, intellectually, and even numerically—if we once again developed a mechanism for social interaction. We need not isolate ourselves in a remote mountain utopia, nor even re-establish the formal network once provided by NBI. But we do need social institutions which allow us to meet with one another.

Perhaps most important of all, how do we live with our families? Rand told us much about rational behavior in romantic relationships, but not all we need to know. Science, in the last few decades, has discovered whole vistas of new facts about the distinctive nature and functions of men and women; about the development of children; and about the structure and value of families. We had better develop the ethical and cultural implications of this knowledge, and on a very practical basis—for if we cannot transmit our values to our children, Objectivism will not have a future.

THE TACTICS OF SANCTION

Ideas are powerful. Rand herself, in her essay 'The New Intellectual', took the position that ideas, and specifically philosophical ideas, determine historical trends. This is a theory calculated to be congenial to intellectuals, 'new' or old; Keynes' famous assertion that politicians are the slaves of dead economists comes to mind. But Rand's theory of history seems incomplete. If the most consistent ideas win out, how did Platonism defeat Aristotelian philosophy? If people accept the wrong ideas at times, what makes them do so?

Perhaps we will eventually come to understand the dynamics of history better. But meanwhile, we must recognize that an idea, no matter how rational, can at best influence society only over the very long run. In view of the urgent need to reverse the current trend toward statism, Objectivists need a more active strategy than 'education' or even leading by example.

The key is Rand's concept of the sanction of the victim. A strike of the mind is, unfortunately, fictional: a tactic which ought to be practical, but isn't. But withdrawing the sanction of the victim offers a general strategy that could have powerful implications.

For, in practical politics, there are certain key pressure-points that exert immense leverage. In politics, as in war, one cannot be strong everywhere; one must concentrate one's forces on the strategic locations. And applying the concept of the sanction of the victim exposes these inconspicuous but crucial issues. As Rand emphasized in *Atlas Shrugged*, a speech supporting the regime from Dagny Taggart is worth a thousand such speeches from famous politicians; the signature of Hank Rearden on a Gift Certificate has more political impact than a battalion of tanks rolling over a protest demonstration. Here is a lesson for us. The greatest danger to our cause comes from deserters— allies who have become morally cowed. When businesses give money to universities and foundations that attack capitalism, for instance, the moral force of their example far outweighs the financial assistance. Whenever and however we may choose to fight, this kind of issue is the where.[5]

THE FIRST OF THEIR RETURN . . .

How will history evaluate Ayn Rand? In a sense, it already has. Her books continue to sell; her ideas continue to excite. In every generation a new crop of teenagers discover *Atlas Shrugged* and find the answers they have been looking for. In *The Fountainhead* Rand compared the public acceptance of Roark's architectural ideas to an underground river; the simile applies as well to her own experience. Though invisible, the acceptance is still there. Though the organized movement shows no progress, millions of people are a little bit better for being exposed to Objectivism.

A hundred years from now, if civilization survives its present crises, Rand will be seen as a giant among twentieth-century thinkers. Not only will Objectivism be recognized as a major contribution to philosophical thought; not only will Rand's ideas be accepted as correct; but very likely our whole way of thinking about philosophy will have changed. Philosophy will be to every thinking person what it was to Rand: not an abstruse subject roughly comparable to Latin grammar in interest and importance, but the fundamental source of right thinking and right action, of crucial, everyday importance.

Strictly as a writer, Rand will certainly be classed among the top ten of her century. Her novels are already classics by any sensible definition, and they will still be read—by high-school students and by college professors alike—when more famous writers of our century are no more than footnotes on yellowing pages. Our descendants will envy us that we were her contemporaries.

NOTES

CHAPTER ONE

1.   Among books attacking Objectivism are the following. Jerome Tuccille's *It Usually Begins with Ayn Rand* is an attempt at a humorous account of the libertarian movement. Albert Ellis's polemic, *Is Objectivism a Religion?*, grew out of his 1968 debate with Nathaniel Branden. More effective is Ellen Plasil's *Therapist*. This story of a young woman who was not only sexually abused but psychologically tormented by her psychotherapist is relevant here because the author implies that Objectivism played a role in her entrapment. She portrays herself and her 'student of Objectivism' friends as repressed, constantly insecure cultists, ripe for ex-ploitation by an unscrupulous 'Objectivist psychotherapist', Dr. Leonard. However, though her account clearly shows the potential for 'Objectivist psychotherapy' to be turned into moral intimidation, Leonard also used—and perverted—other forms of therapy. Ironically, had Plasil been a true 'Randroid' she would have dropped Leonard when he was 'excommunicated' and thus been spared her ordeal.

2.   Murray Rothbard, *The Sociology of the Ayn Rand Cult*.

3.   Nathaniel Branden, *Judgment Day*.

4.   Nathaniel Branden, 'The Benefits and Hazards of the Philosophy of Ayn Rand: A Personal Statement'.

5.   Nathaniel Branden, 'Break Free! An Interview with

Nathaniel Branden'. This lengthy interview provides a useful view of Branden's attitudes during and immediately after his break with Rand.

CHAPTER TWO

1. The only available full biography of Ayn Rand is Barbara Branden's *The Passion of Ayn Rand*, from which most of the following account is abstracted. See the prefatory note to the Bibliography for further discussion.

2. To give just a single example: This was a period in which a scholar of the stature of Ludwig von Mises could not find a regular academic position in the United States.

3. For accounts of 'excommunications', see: Murray Rothbard, 'My Break with Branden and the Rand Cult'; John Hospers, 'Conversations with Ayn Rand'; Tibor Machan, 'Ayn Rand and I'; Rosalie Nichols, 'Confessions of a Randian Cultist'. Rothbard and Hospers, of course, never considered themselves Objectivists.

4. Barbara Branden's account of *l'affaire Branden* has been challenged. No doubt perfect objectivity cannot be expected of one so emotionally involved in the events, but overall her version rings true.

As is so often the case, the participants, including Barbara Branden herself, seem to have overestimated the secrecy of the affair. Rand and the Brandens were the object of concentrated attention from hundreds of New York 'students of Objectivism' who were interested in everything from their musical tastes to what they wore. Under the circumstances, it is not surprising that rumors of a Rand-Branden intimate relationship were circulating long before the 1968 break.

5. During her work on *The Fountainhead* Rand began taking a drug called Dexamyl, a mixture of amphetamine and barbiturate components, believed at the time to boost energy and diminish appetite. She continued to use this prescription medication for decades. The dangers of these mind-altering drugs were not widely recognized until late in Rand's lifetime. Nathaniel Branden (*Judgment Day*, p. 348) suggests the possibility that many

of her emotional difficulties—her bout with depression in the late 1950s, her rages, her irritability—may have been at least partially drug-induced. However, this conjecture is challenged by Barbara Branden (*Passion of Ayn Rand*, pp. 173–74). She points out that the dosages Rand took were low and there is no solid scientific evidence for psychological side-effects at such levels.

CHAPTER THREE

1. Rand's early rejection of Nietzsche is reported by Barbara Branden both in *Who Is Ayn Rand?* (p. 132) and in *The Passion of Ayn Rand* (p. 45). In the latter work (pp. 114–115) Branden discusses the Nietzschean passages in *We the Living* and suggests that Rand really didn't mean it. However, the only evidence she can adduce is Rand's later writings (she quotes *Atlas Shrugged*) on the issue of force.

2. *Thus Spoke Zarathustra*, 'On Those Who Despise the Body'. This and other quotations from Nietzsche are taken from *Nietzsche: An Anthology of His Works*, edited by Otto Manthey-Zorn. Compare this passage with Galt's speech: *Atlas Shrugged*, pp. 1026–1027.

3. Emphasis added. See 'From Ayn Rand's Unpublished Writings: Philosophic Journal (1934)', *The Objectivist Forum*.

4. *Human, All Too Human*, I, 473.

5. *Thus Spoke Zarathustra*, 4.

6. *Human, All Too Human*, I, 483.

7. *Human, All Too Human*, I, 630.

8. *Human, All Too Human*, I, 629.

9. *Beyond Good and Evil*, 229. As Manthey-Zorn puts it (p. 215), "Growth is taken to mean the sublimation of the beast in man. According to the nature of growth it is painful and attended by cruelty." A number of Nietzsche's aphorisms reinforce this point. "Whatever kills me not, makes me stronger." "Spirits and vigor grow through a wound."

10. There is a parallel between Kira's ambition to build bridges out of aluminum, and the Rearden-metal bridge which plays a prominent part in *Atlas Shrugged*.

CHAPTER FOUR

1.   As reported by Barbara Branden: *The Passion of Ayn Rand*, p. 148.

2.   Serge Sookin is deliberately given an alibi by Steve Ingalls. Since only the murderer could have known in advance the time of the murder, Ingalls must be the culprit.

3.   Note an interesting parallel between Kira and Dominique, both of whom initiate romantic relationships with aristocratic 'supermen' by acting as prostitutes. Similarly, in *Penthouse Legend*, Karen Andre's affair with Bjorn Faulkner begins when he attempts to buy her favors for a thousand kroner. Even in *Atlas Shrugged* there is a hint of the same theme, when Rearden and Dagny wish that they had begun their affair in such a way.

4.   While the book is ambiguous about Wynand's suicide, Rand made it explicit in the movie version of *The Fountainhead*.

5.   In a well-known scene in the second chapter of *The Fountainhead*, Roark is asked by Keating whether he should accept a scholarship in Europe or go to work for Guy Francon. Roark chides him for asking advice on such a crucial decision, but recommends taking the job. Keating might have done better not to take Roark's advice—had he gone to the Beaux Arts he would have had a second chance to correct his career choice and become an artist. One wonders if Rand did this intentionally; the ironic illustration of her point might have tickled her fancy.

6.   The book was not published until 1924, and never at all in the Soviet Union, though it may have circulated via *samizdat*. Zamiatin lived in Petrograd during the 1920s, at the same time as Rand; prominent in literary circles, he was a leading anti-Bolshevik intellectual. Rand must surely have been familiar with his work.

CHAPTER FIVE

1.   Rand's Thirty-Six Just are: Hugh Akston, Calvin Atwood, the Brakeman/Music Student, the Chemist, Ken Danagger, Francisco D'Anconia, Quentin Daniels, Ragnar Danneskjold, the Fishwife, John Galt, Richard Halley, Lawrence Hammond, William Hastings, Thomas Hendricks, Owen Kellogg, Kay Ludlow, Roger Marsh, Dick McNamara, Midas Mulligan, the Mine Super-

intendent, Judge Narragansett, Ted Nielsen, the three Professors (who work for McNamára), Hank Rearden, Doug Sanders, the Sculptor, Andrew Stockton, the Taggart Terminal Manager, Dagny Taggart, the Truck Driver (who works for Wyatt), Ellis Wyatt, the Young Mother and her two children. Though Rand makes it clear that there are far more strikers in the valley, only these 36 are identified.

2. A minor though surprising error occurs in the very first pages of the novel. Since when, at the latitude of New York City, does the sun set before 5:00 p.m. on September 2? Surely not even a very irrational government would decree such a weird form of Daylight Savings Time! Another inconsistency appears near the end of the story: With the entire economy in shambles, a few hours before the lights of New York go out, the telephone system is still functioning reliably and Dagny has no trouble finding a working pay phone! It's an ironic tribute to that classic regulated monopoly, Ma Bell.

3. Nathaniel Branden, 'The Benefits and Hazards of the Philosophy of Ayn Rand: A Personal Statement'.

4. Cameron Hawley, *Executive Suite*, p. 247.

5. 'From Ayn Rand's Unpublished Writings: Notes for *Atlas Shrugged*', *The Objectivist Forum*.

6. Ayn Rand, 'About a Woman President', in *The Voice of Reason*, edited by Leonard Peikoff.

7. See *The Passion of Ayn Rand*, pp. 247–248.

8. Mimi Reisel Gladstein, *The Ayn Rand Companion*, p. 67.

9. 'Break Free! An Interview with Nathaniel Branden', *Reason*.

10. Nathaniel Branden, 'Love and Sex in the Philosophy of Ayn Rand'. See also note 3.

11. Barbara Branden also vigorously disagrees with Rand on this issue. See, for instance, her comments in her interview in *Liberty*.

CHAPTER SIX

1. Major papers in this debate are: Nathaniel Branden, 'Rational Egoism'; Tibor Machan, 'A Rationale for Human Rights'; Robert Nozick, 'On the Randian Argument'; Dale E. Lugenbehl, 'The Argument for an Objective Standard of Value'; William

Dwyer, 'The Argument against an Objective Standard of Value'; Tibor Machan, 'Nozick and Rand on Property Rights'; Douglas Den Uyl and Douglas Rasmussen, 'Nozick on the Randian Argument'.

2. For an eloquent indictment of the professoriat by Rand's designated successor, with some 'horror file' material to back it up, see: Leonard Peikoff, 'Assault from the Ivory Tower: The Professors' War against America,' *The Objectivist Forum*.

3. Take for instance *Philosophy: The Basic Issues* (edited by E. D. Klemke, *et al*), which is by no means atypical of philosophy texts. This book provides readings on both sides of major philosophical questions. The only doctrine unchallenged, for which only one side is presented, appears in the Introduction (p. 8):

> [A scientific question] can be settled "once and for all," or at least with a high degree of probability. [A philosophical question] cannot, or at least it is not immediately apparent how it could be.

Another text of readings (W. T. Jones, *et al, Approaches to Ethics*) offers the student this warning up front (p. 14):

> What can the student expect to learn from the study of ethics? He must not expect to absorb a conception of the good life, or a ready-made code of conduct, in the manner that the student of physics can absorb a knowledge of Newtonian mechanics and the differential calculus.

4. Mortimer Adler, *Reforming Education*, p. xxix.

5. For a more extensive discussion of this position, and paraphrases from Aristotle and several other philosophers, see Douglas J. Den Uyl and Douglas B. Rassmussen, *The Philosophic Thought of Ayn Rand*, pp. 4–5.

6. Leonard Peikoff, '"Maybe You're Wrong"', *The Objectivist Forum*.

7. 'From Ayn Rand's Unpublished Writings: Philosophic Notes', *The Objectivist Forum*.

8. The analytic-synthetic dichotomy has been criticized by Willard Quine, John Wild, Morton White, Wallace Matson, and others.

9. Thomas S. Kuhn, *The Structure of Scientific Revolutions*. Rand does not specifically mention Kuhn. I bring his name into

the discussion because his work (which is erudite and full of important insights) has been used so widely to attack science's claim to certainty. His model of scientific progress, at least in the vulgar form which has been so enormously influential, would seem to fit precisely the line of argument which Rand criticizes in this passage. On p. 170 Kuhn suggests:

> We may, to be more precise, have to relinquish the notion, explicit or implicit, that changes of paradigm carry scientists and those who learn from them closer and closer to the truth.

In defending himself from critics Kuhn later (p. 206) makes his position quite clear. Science *does* make a meaningless sort of progress in that its repertoire of "puzzle-solutions" grows. But it is *not* the case that "successive theories grow ever closer to, or approximate more and more closely to, the truth."

Kuhn's position is rooted in his belief that concepts are not open-ended and that unexpected discoveries must inevitably invalidate prior concepts; see p. 127. This is just the argument that Rand is attacking in this passage.

It should be noted that Kuhn emphatically does not regard himself as a positivist, and indeed attacks logical positivism (pp. 95–103) for defending the idea of scientific progress by claiming that new theories may subsume the older ones they replace.

For a thorough discussion of the issues raised by Kuhn, see Larry Laudan, *Science and Relativism*.

10. Ayn Rand, *Introduction to Objectivist Epistemology* (Second edn.), p. 67.

11. Kuhn's historical material actually supports Rand's theory of concepts better than it supports his own. Contrary to Kuhn's model, a particular science does not undergo an infinite series of 'paradigm shifts'. Instead, each field of science typically experiences two shifts. The first is the shift from pure superstition to pseudoscience; the second from pseudoscience to true science.

Take planetary astronomy, Kuhn's most famous example. This discipline began as astrology, when ancient people observed that certain stars changed their position in the sky and called them 'wanderers' or 'planets'. This unaccountable behavior was explained by identifying the planets with gods. The first 'paradigm shift' created Ptolemaic astronomy, which fit the planets into a mechanical model and thus began the effort at what we would now call a scientific explanation. But superstition retained an influence; it was required that Earth, the home of man, be at the center of the universe, and that planetary orbits be 'perfect' circles. The Copernican/Keplerian paradigm shift established planetary astronomy as a true science by eliminating both of these residues of superstition. And that is the end of paradigm shifts for this area of science; we may be quite sure that no future revolution will ever occur, and that if students are still taught astronomy a million years from now they will learn, as they do today, that the planets move around the sun in (approximate) ellipses.

Of course, other fields of science tend to go through a similar three-stage process. Thus alchemy (superstition) gave way to the phlogiston theory (pseudoscience) which in turn gave way to the modern field of chemistry with elements, mass conservation, and valence. In biology, creationism was supplanted by Lamarckism, and that by Darwinism.

Kuhn's argument depends on confusing real scientific revolutions of this type with 'revolutions' in which the new paradigm extends science into a new field of inquiry, and the old paradigm is delimited but not replaced.

12. Today more than ever before scientists are harassed by the need for epistemological guidance. As experiments become more complex and difficult to interpret, their meaning becomes less immediately clear. Furthermore, much of modern science, particularly mathematics and physics, deals with explicitly epistemological questions. Both relativistic dynamics and quantum mechanics, for instance, make specific assertions about limits on what is knowable, and raise problems which border on paradox.

13. Strictly speaking this is a modern formulation of the problem of ethics, dating from relatively recent philosophical skeptics such as Hume. The ancients would not have recognized the 'ought-from-is' problem as a problem. Of course a number of philosophers besides Rand have rejected Hume's argument; for just one example, see John R. Searle, 'How to Derive "Ought" from "Is"'.

14. Ayn Rand, *For the New Intellectual*, p. 13.

15. Ayn Rand, *For the New Intellectual*, p. 147. It is important to

understand that a value is not something one desires or wants, but something one acts to achieve. One wonders whether Rand was familiar with the work of Ralph Barton Perry. He conceived of 'value' along the same lines as Rand, and was led thereby to propose a "bio-centric" theory of value. (See Ralph Barton Perry, *General Theory of Value*.)

16. Notably by Hospers (*Introduction to Philosophical Analysis* [Second Ed.], p. 594) and by Lugenbehl; see note 1.

17. Ayn Rand, *The Virtue of Selfishness*, pp. 16–17. A paper by Eric Mack—'How to Derive Ethical Egoism'—which attempts to exploit the 'ultimate end' approach, further points up the difficulties involved in doing so.

18. It is sometimes argued that non-living entities, such as target-seeking missiles, have 'goals'. This position is refuted at length by Harry Binswanger in his *The Biological Basis of Teleological Concepts*. The question of volition remains vexed, but determinists open themselves to 'stolen concept' charges. Although ethical relativists have often denied the possibility of an 'ultimate end', they have in doing so repudiated the possibility of real values.

19. If we look at the more general context the situation becomes even worse. Reproduction is extremely hazardous for many animals, and fatal for some. Consider, for instance, insect species in which the male is eaten by the female immediately after, or even during, copulation; or those in which the female's body becomes the initial food for her offspring. These cases—fortunately!—have no direct relevance to human ethics, but they certainly make hash of Rand's general claim that an organism's survival is the only possible 'end in itself'.

In general Rand and her followers have tiptoed around the question of reproduction and human valuing of children. Binswanger does approach the issue, very obliquely, in dealing with a problem of teleology (how can an action, the effect, precede the goal, the cause?) See Binswanger, *The Biological Basis of Teleological Concepts*, pp 156–58 and pp 165–66.

20. Binswanger, *The Biological Basis of Teleological Concepts*, p. 165.

21. Binswanger, *The Biological Basis of Teleological Concepts*, pp. 64–65. Perry appears to conceive of life in a very similar way, and

his 'moralization of life' operates along lines evocative of John Galt's "Happiness is a state of non-contradictory joy." See Ralph Barton Perry, *Realms of Value*.

22. Jack Wheeler, 'Rand and Aristotle: A Comparison of Objectivist and Aristotelian Ethics', in *The Philosophic Thought of Ayn Rand*, p. 81.

23. Cf. David Hume, *Treatise of Human Nature*, p. 469.

24. This observation is of course not original. See for instance Tibor Machan, *Introduction to Philosophical Inquiries*, p. 186.

25. Ayn Rand, *Atlas Shrugged*, p. 451.

26. Ayn Rand, *Atlas Shrugged*, p. 1118.

27. 'Aha! So a skillful bank robber is acting morally!' This is to confuse efficacy with efficiency. To be skillful, a surgeon must not only make incisions well; he must make them in the right places!

Obviously there are many choices which are morally trivial in an economic sense—that is, one's cost of determining the optimum course of action is less than the difference in benefit between the best and worst courses of action.

28. In fact, it might be helpful to establish a trichotomy: life, death, and 'negative life'—analogous to negative numbers—a status in which a person can achieve no values and in which any action merely makes the situation worse.

29. The definition of 'life' raises some fascinating and important questions. Are the electromechanical devices described in *Vehicles* by Valentino Braitenberg, which in spite of their simple construction are capable of amazingly complex goal-directed behavior, 'alive'? We may say they are not, since they are human constructs, not organisms. But then what of a new micro-organism constructed by gene-splicing?

Note that we must make a distinction between 'life' as a characteristic of an organism, and 'life' as a biological phenomenon in general. It is the first sense of the term that we have used in the context of our discussion of ethics. But also relevant is the second sense. Probably the most widely accepted definition of 'life' in a biological context is that proposed by Jacques Monod (see his *Chance and Necessity*). He cites three essential characteristics of living organisms: goal-directed behavior; self-constructing action; and reproduction. This definition of life in biological context does have implications for objectivist ethics; if we accept that reproduction is part of the concept of 'life', we have a tool with which to remove the objectivist ethics' difficulties with moral issues involving children.

30. In doing this we do not abandon the 'either-or' dichotomy between life and death. The dichotomy between 'nothing' and 'something' remains, even when we recognize that there may be different levels or quantities of 'something'.

31. Ayn Rand, *The Virtue of Selfishness*, p. 47.

32. Eric Mack, 'The Fundamental Moral Elements of Rand's Theory of Rights', in *The Philosophic Thought of Ayn Rand* (edited by Den Uyl and Rasmussen), p. 139.

33. David Friedman, 'Simple Principles vs. the Real World'.

34. J. Charles King, 'Life and the Theory of Value: The Randian Argument Reconsidered', in *The Philosophic Thought of Ayn Rand* (edited by Den Uyl and Rasmussen), pp. 117-118.

35. Robert Nozick, 'On the Randian Argument'.

36. Ayn Rand, 'The Objectivist Ethics', in *The Virtue of Selfishness*, p. 22.

37. Nathaniel Branden, in *Who is Ayn Rand?*, p. 30.

38. Ayn Rand, 'The Psycho-Epistemology of Art', in *The Romantic Manifesto*, p. 22. This position is formally inconsistent with Rand's general principal that all human action has moral significance. And, if we accept the testimony of Barbara Branden and Nathaniel Branden, Rand did not hold to this in practice but frequently pronounced moral judgment on people based on their tastes in art.

39. Rand's views on Beethoven are reported by Barbara Branden: *The Passion of Ayn Rand*, p. 243, 311. Her views on Wagner were expressed in conversation with me.

40. Ayn Rand, 'What is Romanticism?', in *The Romantic Manifesto*, p. 74.

41. *ibid.*, p. 66.

CHAPTER SEVEN

1. Barbara Branden, *The Passion of Ayn Rand*, pp. 203–05.

2. For a discussion of the conservative reaction to *Atlas Shrugged*, see George H. Nash, *The Conservative Intellectual Move-*

ment in America, pp. 156–58. (This book also provides an excellent introduction to the general history of postwar conservatism.) Conservatives like to dismiss objectivism as a fringe cult, never important and now extinct (see for instance 'Ayn Rand is Dead,' *National Review*, May 28, 1990, p. 35). However, their professed unconcern is belied by their inability to stop taking shots at Rand. Recently, for instance, *National Review* (April 30, 1990, p. 54) felt that appearance of the second edition of *Introduction to Objectivist Epistemology* merited book review space for another maliciously inaccurate attack. One gets the impression of frightened urchins poking Rand's body with sticks to reassure themselves that she's really dead. They are in for a shock.

3.   Ayn Rand, 'Conservatism: An Obituary', in *Capitalism: The Unknown Ideal*, p. 192.

4.   Ayn Rand, 'The Anatomy of a Compromise', in *Capitalism: The Unknown Ideal*, p. 146.

5.   Rand cannot claim sole credit, however. A revival of the ideas of the Austrian economist Joseph Schumpeter has given a major boost to modern theories of entrepreneurship.

6.   For thorough-going defenses of the anarcho-capitalist position, see: Murray Rothbard, *For a New Liberty*; David Friedman, *The Machinery of Freedom*, Second Edition; Morris and Linda Tannehill, *The Market for Liberty*; Richard and Ernestine Perkins, *Rational Anarchy*.

7.   Locke himself suggested that the people might prudently leave default powers—what he called 'prerogative'—in the hands of government (specifically, the Executive), in order to allow for unforeseen contingencies. Chapter XIV of the *Second Treatise of Government* discusses the pros and cons of prerogative. However, he was quite explicit that all governmental authority derives from the consent of the governed, and that if the people are not entirely confident of their rulers' discretion they may, and should, limit or eliminate the 'prerogative'; see paragraphs 163 and 164.

This concept of the default of powers or 'prerogative' is crucial to American constitutional theory. It is most clearly brought out in the debate over the meaning of the Ninth Amendment. For a thorough discussion, see Randy E. Barnett (ed.), *The Rights Retained by the People*.

8.   Ayn Rand, 'The Nature of Government', in *The Virtue of Selfishness*, p. 107; see especially pp. 112–13. This article, written in 1963, was merely an opening salvo in a debate which continues unabated to this day. There exists a copious literature on the merits of anarcho-libertarianism. Tibor Machan and John Hospers have been prominent opponents; Murray Rothbard its most famous supporter.

9.   In fact, there are cases where two governments have existed within the same geographical area without conflict. Perhaps the best example is Hong Kong, where for over a century there have been two separate legal systems, one for Chinese and one for British inhabitants. Of course, technically these systems are subordinate to a single government, but functionally they are themselves governments. They do not, however, 'compete' in the sense discussed by anarcho-capitalists, since in general a citizen has no choice as to which system governs him.

Another example is provided by the situation in the United States, where state and local police sometimes become involved in jurisdictional disputes with the FBI, our national police force. Similarly, there is much debate and occasional conflict over the jurisdictional privileges of state versus federal courts.

10.   Ayn Rand, 'The Missing Link', in *Philosophy: Who Needs It*, p. 43.

11.   Peter Schwartz, 'Libertarianism: The Perversion of Liberty', in *The Voice of Reason* (edited by Leonard Peikoff), p. 311.

12.   I am here using 'social contract' primarily in the sense of an agreement between citizens and government, not necessarily in the rather broader context intended by Rousseau. Perhaps 'political contract' would be more accurate. It should be noted that Locke was wary of the concept of a 'contract' between people and State, preferring to speak in terms of a "trust".

13.   Ayn Rand, 'Government Financing in a Free Society', in *The Virtue of Selfishness*, p. 116.

14.   This is said to be a quote from Plato's *Republic*. Talk about the Miracle of the Rose!

15.   One should note that those cultures which have been distinguished by limited government, close to laissez-faire economies, and few legal restrictions on personal freedom, have also

exhibited strong social and moral restrictions on their people. Victorian England provides a good example. This correlation deserves systematic study.

CHAPTER EIGHT

1.   I must confess to an occasional ambivalence on the question of 'excommunication'. Certainly I moan with disgust when bell, book, and candle are wielded against an Edith Efron or a David Kelley. But then I cringe when the media describe some scoundrel (such as convicted spy Jerry Whitworth) as "an admirer of Ayn Rand". To quote Midas Mulligan, "Boy! — what a temptation it was, I can almost see why people do it."

2.   *Reason* 20(1), May 1988. See especially Robert Poole's article, 'Things Are a Lot Groovier Now', on p. 48.

3.   As this is written, the Soviet Union and its satellites are caught up in a fervent tide of democratic reform. The new regimes, assuming they survive, seem to seek a slightly modified form of communism, or at most a Swedish-style welfare state, rather than laissez-faire. But we may hope.

4.   A somewhat similar argument has recently been made by L. H. Rockwell, Jr. in *Liberty* ('The Case for Paleolibertarianism'). He arrives from a traditional Christian viewpoint, rather than Objectivism (to which he is hostile), and seeks an alliance with elements of conservatism.

5.   Indeed, Rand's last public speech, read posthumously at the Ford Hall Forum by Leonard Peikoff, was devoted to the sanction of the victim.

BIBLIOGRAPHY

Obviously the most important sources for this book are the writings of Ayn Rand herself. The Rand canon has been augmented by her 'official' successors, Leonard Peikoff and Harry Binswanger, and I have drawn on their work where it helps to illuminate certain difficult arguments. In accessing Rand's key concepts I frequently found helpful Binswanger's excellent chrestomathy, *The Ayn Rand Lexicon*.

In discussion of Ayn Rand's ideas, some difficulty arises with regard to the pre-schism writings of Nathaniel and Barbara Branden. Rand never actually repudiated these articles and lectures and there is no reason to believe that she came to disagree with them in any substantial way. Furthermore, in view of the intimate intellectual intercourse between Rand and the Brandens during the period in which they were written, one may assume that Rand contributed significant creative input to them. However, they occupy a rather uncertain position in the 'official' Objectivist literature. For this and other reasons I have chosen to avoid discussion of the topics in psychology (including 'psycho-epistemology', 'social metaphysics', and so on) with which they are chiefly concerned. These issues are neither uninteresting nor unimportant, but I am not prepared at this time to attempt their integration with the main body of Ayn Rand's thinking. I have, however, quoted works from this group when it appeared essential to clarify a key point.

There is a considerable literature of philosophical debate on Objectivism. Some of this material has been cited in the text, particularly the essays in Den Uyl and Rasmussen's *The Philosophical Thought of Ayn Rand*. I also found very useful the critiques and interpretive writings of Tibor Machan, John Hospers, and David Kelley. Other works, such as James T. Baker's analysis, offer nothing of value; even his errors are not instructive. I have not attempted to compile an exhaustive bibliography on Ayn Rand; for more extensive coverage of the literature, readers should consult Mimi Gladstein's *The Ayn Rand Companion*.

It should also be stressed again that this book is not a biography of Rand, nor a history of her times, and that those portions of the text bearing on these topics exist only to provide a context for discussion of her ideas. For biographical information about Rand, I have, of necessity, relied heavily on Barbara Branden's *The Passion of Ayn Rand*. I also found useful her 'authorized' sketch of Rand's career in *Who Is Ayn Rand?* I drew further biographical facts from Nathaniel Branden's memoir, *Judgment Day*, exercising due caution since his book is a personal defense—a lawyer's brief, so to speak—rather than an impartial account. Also a partisan document is Virginia L. L. Hamel's *In Defense of Ayn Rand*; while sympathetic to some of her arguments, I do not think she makes a compelling case against the general factual accuracy of the Brandens' narratives. Personal accounts by other people who knew Rand, such as John Hospers, provided additional information.

For general historical information on the American Right I have drawn on a wide variety of texts. George Nash's *The Conservative Intellectual Movement in America* provides a comprehensive survey of the development of modern conservatism. Unfortunately, for the libertarian movement no such useful overview is available, though Jan Narveson's *The Libertarian Idea* does provide some coverage of various libertarian approaches.

In analyzing the influence of Friedrich Nietzsche on Rand's thinking I encountered considerable difficulty. This philosopher is notoriously obscure—it sometimes seems that any quotation can be offset with another which apparently contradicts it—and commentators often disagree on what Nietzsche 'really meant to say'. I have been guided to a great extent by the interpretation presented by Otto Manthey-Zorn. I also found useful *The Philosophy of Friedrich Nietzsche* by H. L. Mencken, which offers an unusually clear exposition of Nietzsche's doctrines.

A few words on quotations and footnotes: I have not felt it necessary to quote extensively from Ayn Rand's writings, as it is assumed that the reader already has a basic familiarity with her work. I have also used only sparingly 'horror file' quotes and references. Many Objectivist writers make heavy use of this expedient, as a sort of pre-emptive strike against the inevitable response from slippery opponents that 'no one believes' the unbelievable and 'no one denies' the undeniable. To my mind, this whole game is rather silly. It is quite clear where thinkers like Hume, Kant, and Kuhn really stand, in spite of the protective blasts of the philosophical Venticelli: 'Nobody believes *that* in the world!' However, in response to editorial prodding, I have inserted documentation for some particularly egregious thoughtcrimes.

Adler, Mortimer. *Ten Philosophical Mistakes.* New York: Collier, 1985.

———. *Reforming Education.* New York: Macmillan, 1988.

Baker, James T. *Ayn Rand.* Boston: Twayne, 1987.

Barnett, Randy E., ed. *The Rights Retained by the People.* Fairfax, Virginia: George Mason University Press, 1989.

Binswanger, Harry. *The Biological Basis of Teleological Concepts.* Los Angeles: Ayn Rand Institute Press, 1990.

———, ed. *The Ayn Rand Lexicon.* New York: New American Library, 1986.

Braitenberg, Valentino. *Vehicles.* Cambridge: MIT Press, 1984.

Branden, Barbara. *The Passion of Ayn Rand.* New York: Doubleday, 1986.

———. 'Barbara Branden Speaks Out'. *Liberty* 3 (3), 49 (1990).

Branden, Barbara, and Branden, Nathaniel. *Who Is Ayn Rand?*. New York: Paperback Library, 1962.

Branden, Nathaniel. 'Rational Egoism', *Personalist* 51, 196; 305 (1970).

―――. 'Break Free! An Interview with Nathaniel Branden', *Reason*, October 1971, p. 4.

―――. 'The Benefits and Hazards of the Philosophy of Ayn Rand: A Personal Statement' (taped lecture). New York: Laissez Faire Books, 1982.

―――. 'Love and Sex in the Philosophy of Ayn Rand' (taped lecture). New York: Laissez Faire Books, 1983.

―――. *Judgment Day*. Boston: Houghton Mifflin, 1989.

Chambers, Whittaker. 'Big Sister Is Watching You'. *National Review* 1957, 594.

Den Uyl, Douglas J., and Rasmussen, Douglas B. 'Nozick on the Randian Argument', *Personalist* 59, 184 (1978).

―――, eds. *The Philosophic Thought of Ayn Rand*. Chicago: University of Illinois Press, 1984.

Dwyer, William. 'The Argument against an Objective Standard of Value', *Personalist* 55, 165 (1974).

Ellis, Albert. *Is Objectivism a Religion?* New York: Lyle Stuart, 1968.

Friedman, David. *The Machinery of Freedom* (2nd Edition). La Salle, Illinois: Open Court, 1989.

―――. 'Simple Principles vs. the Real World', *Liberty* 3(1), 37 (1989).

Gladstein, Mimi Reisel. *The Ayn Rand Companion*. Westport, Connecticut: Greenwood Press, 1984.

Hamel, Virginia L.L. *In Defense of Ayn Rand*. Brookline, Massachusetts: New Beacon Publications, 1990.

Hawley, Cameron. *Executive Suite*. Boston: Houghton-Mifflin, 1952.

―――. *Cash McCall*. Boston: Houghton-Mifflin, 1955.

―――. *The Lincoln Lords*. Boston: Little, Brown, 1960.

Hospers, John. *Introduction to Philosophical Analysis* (Second edition). Englewood Cliffs, NJ: Prentice-Hall, 1967.

———. 'Conversations with Ayn Rand'. *Liberty* 4(1), 42 (1990).

Hume, David. *Treatise of Human Nature.* Oxford: Oxford University Press, 1978.

Jones, W. T., *et al*, eds. *Approaches to Ethics.* New York: McGraw-Hill, 1969.

Kelley, David. *The Evidence of the Senses: A Realist Theory of Perception.* Baton Rouge, Louisiana: Louisiana State University Press, 1986.

Klemke, E. D., Kline, A. David, and Hollinger, Robert, eds. *Philosophy: The Basic Issues.* New York: St. Martin's Press, 1986.

Kuhn, Thomas S. *The Structure of Scientific Revolutions* (Second edition). Chicago: University of Chicago Press, 1970.

Laudan, Larry. *Science and Relativism.* Chicago: University of Chicago Press, 1990.

Locke, John. Two Treatises of Government. Cambridge: Cambridge University Press, 1967.

Lugenbehl, Dale E. 'The Argument for an Objective Standard of Value', *Personalist* 55, 155 (1974).

Machan, Tibor. 'A Rationale for Human Rights'. *Personalist* 52, 216 (1971).

———. *Human Rights and Human Liberties.* Chicago: Nelson Hall, 1975.

———. 'Nozick and Rand on Property Rights'. *Personalist* 58, 192 (1977).

———. *Introduction to Philosophical Inquiries.* New York: University Press of America, 1985.

———. *Individuals and Their Rights.* La Salle, Illinois: Open Court, 1989.

———. 'Ayn Rand and I'. *Liberty* 3 (2), 49 (1989).

Mack, Eric. 'How to Derive Ethical Egoism'. *Personalist* 52, 736 (1971).

Manthey-Zorn, Otto, ed. *Nietzsche: An Anthology of His Works.* New York: Washington Square Press, 1964.

Mencken, Henry L. *The Philosophy of Friedrich Nietzsche.* Torrance, California: Noontide Press, 1982.

Merwin, Samuel, and Webster. *Calumet 'K'.* New York: NBI Press, 1967.

Monod, Jacques. *Chance and Necessity.* New York: Knopf, 1971.

Narveson, Jan. *The Libertarian Idea.* Philadelphia: Temple University Press, 1988.

Nash, George H. *The Conservative Intellectual Movement in America.* New York: Basic Books, 1976

Nichols, Rosalie. 'Confessions of a Randian Cultist'. Brian Eeningenburg, 1972.

Nozick, Robert. 'On the Randian Argument'. *Personalist* 52, 282 (1971).

Peikoff, Leonard. '"Maybe You're Wrong"'. *The Objectivist Forum* 2 (2), 8 (1981).

———. *The Ominous Parallels.* New York: New American Library, 1982.

———. 'Assault from the Ivory Tower: The Professor's War against America'. *The Objectivist Forum* 4 (5), 1; (6), 9 (1983).

——— ed. *The Early Ayn Rand.* New York: New American Library, 1984.

——— ed. *The Voice of Reason.* New York: New American Library, 1988.

Perkins, Richard and Perkins, Ernestine. *Rational Anarchy.* St. Thomas, Ontario: Phibbs Printing World, 1971.

Perry, Ralph Barton. *General Theory of Value.* Cambridge, Massachusetts: Harvard University Press, 1926.

——. *Realms of Value*. Cambridge, Massachusetts: Harvard University Press, 1954.

Plasil, Ellen. *Therapist*. New York: St. Martin's Press, 1985.

Poole, Robert, Jr. 'Things Are a Lot Groovier Now'. *Reason* 20 (1), May 1988, p. 48.

Rand, Ayn. *We the Living* (First edition). New York: Macmillan, 1936.

——. *We the Living* (Revised edition). New York: Random House, 1959.

——. *We the Living* (movie version, videotape). New York: Angelika Films, 1988.

——. *The Night of January Sixteenth*. New York: Longmans, Green, 1936.

——. *The Night of January Sixteenth* (amateur edition, Nathaniel Edward Reeid, ed.). New York: David McKay, undated.

——. *The Night of January Sixteenth* (authorized edition). New York: World Publishing, 1968.

——. *The Fountainhead*. New York: Bobbs-Merrill, 1943.

——. *The Fountainhead* (movie version, videotape). Culver City, California: MGM/UA Home Video, 1990.

——. *Anthem*. New York: New American Library, 1946.

——. *Atlas Shrugged*. New York: Random House, 1957.

——. *For the New Intellectual*; New York: Random House, 1961.

——. *Capitalism: The Unknown Ideal*. New York, New American Library, 1967.

——. *The Romantic Manifesto*. New York: New American Library, 1971.

——. *The Virtue of Selfishness*. New York: New American Library, 1974.

——. *Philosophy: Who Needs It*. New York: Bobbs-Merrill, 1982.

————. 'From Ayn Rand's Unpublished Writings: Philosophic Journal (1934)'. *The Objectivist Forum* 4 (4), 1 (1983).

————. 'From Ayn Rand's Unpublished Writings: Notes for *Atlas Shrugged*'. *The Objectivist Forum* 4 (6), 1 (1983).

————. 'From Ayn Rand's Unpublished Writings: Philosophic Notes'. *The Objectivist Forum* 5 (4), 1 (1984).

————. *Introduction to Objectivist Epistemology* (Second edition); New York: NAL Books, 1990.

Rockwell, L.H., Jr. 'The Case for Paleolibertarianism'. *Liberty* 3 (3), 34 (1990).

Rockwell, L.H., Jr., and Tucker, Jeffrey A. 'Ayn Rand Is Dead'. *National Review* 1990 (5/28), 35.

Rothbard, Murray. *Man, Economy, and State*. Princeton, New Jersey: Van Nostrand, 1962.

————. *For a New Liberty*. New York: Macmillan, 1973.

————. *The Sociology of the Ayn Rand Cult*. Port Townsend, WA: Liberty Publishing, 1987.

————. 'My Break with Branden and the Rand Cult', *Liberty* 3 (1), 27 (1989).

Searle, John R. 'How to Derive "Ought" from "Is"'. *Philosophical Review* 73 , 43 (1964).

Tannehill, Morris and Tannehill, Linda. *The Market for Liberty*. Lansing, Michigan: no publisher given, 1970.

Tuccille, Jerome. *It Usually Begins with Ayn Rand*. New York: Stein and Day, 1972.

Veatch, Henry. *Rational Man: A Modern Interpretation of Aristotelian Ethics*. Bloomington, Indiana: Indiana University Press, 1962.

————. *Human Rights: Fact or Fancy?* Baton Rouge, Louisiana: Louisiana State University Press, 1985.

Zamiatin, Yevgeny. *We*. New York: Dutton, 1924.

INDEX

Adler, Mortimer, 89, 154
aesthetics, *see* esthetics
alienation of the good, 15–16, 43, 54–55, 84–85
altruism
  as morality based on death, 85, 100
  Nietzsche's rejection of, 22, 23–24
analytic-synthetic dichotomy, 96–97
anarcho-capitalism
  as purest form of libertarianism, 135–36
  free rider problem and, 138–39
  social contract theory attacked by, 140–41, 146
  see also libertarianism
Anthem, 12, 56–57
Aristotle, 88, 90–91, 105, 110, 124, 144
art, *see* esthetics
Atlas Shrugged, 18, 91, 145
  heroes in, 66–68, 74, 76–78
  Jewish symbolism in, 61–62
  lawnmower and, 2–3
  philosophical integration in, 63–66
  plot structure of, 62–63
  publication of, 13
  reactions to, 1, 13, 130
  style of, 59–61
  villains in, 75–76

Austrian economics, 133, 140
axiomatic concepts, 95
Ayn Rand Letter, The, 15, 147

Binswanger, Harry, 4, 103, 154, 173 n18, 173 n19, 179
Block, Walter, 139
Bork, Robert, 137
Branden, Barbara, 166–67 n5, 169 n11
  attitude toward Rand of, 166 n4
  biography of Rand by, 5, 166 n1, 180
  opinion on Nietzscheanism of Rand, 167 n1
  pre-schism writings of, 179
Branden, Nathaniel, 88, 138, 166–67 n5
  affair with Ayn Rand of, 5, 14
  attitude toward Objectivism of, 4–5, 180
  attitude toward Rand of, 7
  criticisms of Rand from, 79–84
  founding of NBI by, 14
  new field of ethics suggested by, 121–22
  pre-schism writings of, 179
Buckley, William F., 13, 130

Calumet K, 66–67
career choice, 82

Cash McCall, 67
certainty, 91–92
Chambers, Whittaker, 130
Chodorov, Frank, 135
concept-formation, 93–98
conservatism
    development of modern, 132–33
    Objectivist attack on, 133–34
conservative movement, 12
    influence of Objectivism on, 2, 131–32
    libertarian elements in, 131–32
    opposition to Objectivism by, 14, 130, 176 n2

'D'Anconia, Francisco Domingo Carlos Andres Sebastian' 71–72, 79
definitions, 93–95, 124–25

Efron, Edith, 14, 178 n1
egoism
    criminals' alleged practice of, 114–16
    Nietzsche's attitude and, 24
    Objectivist vs. other versions of, 113
    political implications of, 145
emotional repression, *see* repression
environmentalism, 157
epistemology
    analytic-synthetic dichotomy and, 96–97
    anti–relativism in Objectivist, 91–93
    axiomatic concepts in, 95
    certainty and Objectivist, 91–92
    concept theory of Objectivism for, 93–98
    induction and deduction in, 96–97
    nominalism and realism in, 94–95
    science and, 97–98, 170–71 n9, 171–72 n11, 172 n12
    skepticism in, 88–90, 92, 96–97
'Escort', 29
esthetics
    definition of art by Rand for, 122
    ethical considerations and, 122
    musical, 124–25

redefinition of art for Objectivist, 124–25
    sense of life in, 122–25
ethics
    argument from ends-in-themselves in, 102
    argument from means-in-themselves in, 104–05
    Aristotelean, 105
    bio-centric approach to, 118–120, 121
    criminality as challenge to Objectivist, 114–16, 174 n27
    definition of morality and, 99
    emergencies as challenge to Objectivist, 113–15
    epistemological and metaphysical arguments for Objectivist, 100–01
    esthetic issues and, 122
    laziness as challenge to Objectivist, 116–17
    life as basis of Objectivist, 99–105, 109–112, 174–75 n29, 175 n30
    normative statements from, 106–07
    'ought from is' problem of, 98, 100, 106–09, 172 n13
    political implications of, 146–47
    pride in Objectivist, 119–120
    productivity in Objectivist, 119
    rationality in Objectivist, 119
    reproduction as issue in, 103, 120–21 173 n19, 174 n29
    self-improvement in Objectivist, 114, 115, 116–17, 119–120
    skepticism in, 100, 106–08
    suicide and Objectivist, 110–11
    values and, 99–101
    see also egoism
'excommunication', 3, 14, 152, 178 n1
Executive Suite, 67–68

feminism
    as statist ideology, 157
    Rand's attitude toward, 69–71, 121
Fountainhead, The, 21, 25
    despair as theme of, 46, 48, 54
    publication of, 12–13

structure of, 45–47, 53–54
'Vesta Dunning' passages of, 48, 53
'Francon, Dominique', 43, 46–50, 68
free rider problem, 138–39
Friedman, David, 115
Friedman, Milton, 139

'Galt, John', 62, 73–74, 79
Gilder, George, 2, 13, 134
Gladstein, Mimi, 78
Goldwater, Barry, 130–31
'Good Copy', 28
Gotthelf, Allan, 4
government
    competition between, 138, 177 n9
    default powers or prerogative of,
        137, 176 n7
    financing of, 140, 143–44
    Objectivist theory of, 142–47
    origin of, 136–37, 141
    see also politics

Hawley, Cameron, 67–68
Hayek, Friedrich von, 13, 133
Hazlitt, Henry, 129
'Her Second Career', 29
Hobbes, Thomas, 136–37, 146
Hospers, John, 14, 154
Hugo, Victor, 27, 34, 36
Hume, David, 96, 105–06
'Husband I Bought, The', 28

Ibsen, Henrik, 27
Ideal, 41–44
independence, 47, 50–51
induction, 96–97
Introduction to Objectivist Epistemology,
    87, 93–98

Kant, Immanuel, 22, 52, 96–97
'Keating, Peter', 50–51
Kelley, David, 154, 178 n1
King, J. Charles, 116
Koestler, Arthur, 122
Kuhn, Thomas, 97, 170–71 n9, 171–
    72 n11

Lane, Rose Wilder, 129
Lefevre, Robert, 135
liberalism, 13, 137
libertarian movement
    conservative movement and, 131–32
    development of, 135
    Objectivist influence on, 6
    strategy of, 148–49, 156–57
Libertarian Party, 155–56
libertarianism
    anarcho-capitalism as purest form of,
        135–36
    definition of, 135–36, 140
    ideological obsolescence of, 156–57
    Objectivist attack on, 137–140
    subjectivism characteristic of, 139–
        140, 147, 148–49, 158
    see also anarcho-capitalism
life
    definition of, 103–04, 110–11,
        174 n29, 175 n30
    of man qua man, 109–112
lifeboat arguments, 113–14
Locke, John, 136–37, 141, 144, 146,
    176 n7

Machan, Tibor, 88, 154
Mack, Eric, 114, 115, 173 n17
meta-ethics, 99
metaphysical value-judgments, 122–23
metaphysics, 90–91
mind-body dichotomy
    hierarchical rejection of, 95
    rejection by Nietzsche and Rand of,
        22–23
Mises, Ludwig von, 13, 129, 166 n2
Montesquieu, Charles de Secondat,
    Baron de, 146
morality, see ethics
Murray, Charles, 2
music, 124–25

NBI (Nathaniel Branden Institute), 3,
    14–15, 87, 89, 151–53, 160
Nietzsche, Friedrich, 180–81
    cruelty in philosophy of, 25–26

influence on Ayn Rand, 8–9, 17, 21–26
reason and emotion for, 23
'superman' concept of, 23–25
Naturalism, 123
Night of January Sixteenth, The, see
    Penthouse Legend
Nock, Albert J., 129
nominalism, 93–95
normative statements, 106–07
Novak, Michael, 134
Nozick, Robert, 88, 117–18, 154

Objectivism
    development of, 17
    opposition to, 2, 130
    see also specific philosophical subjects
        such as ethics
Objectivist movement, 2, 14
    academic philosophers and, 153–55
    characterized as cult, 2–5
    complacency of, 157, 159–160
    organization of, 151–53
    renunciation of political action by,
        131–32
    schism in, 5, 14–15, 159–160
Objectivist psychotherapy, 121, 165 n1
Objectivist The, and *Objectivist Newsletter,*
    The, 14, 87
O'Connor, Frank, 15, 70–71

para–ethics, 121–22
Paterson, Isabel, 13, 129
Peikoff, Leonard, 96, 154, 170 n2, 179
Penthouse Legend (The Night of January
    Sixteenth) 18
    appearance of, 12
    editions of, 30–31
    Nietzschean ideas in, 31–32
Perry, Ralph Barton, 172–73 n15,
    173 n21
philosophy
    academic discipline of, 87–90
    purpose and value of, 88
    see also epistemology; ethics; meta-
        physics; Objectivism

politics
    basic issue of, 136–37
    ethical basis for, 146–47
    Objectivist withdrawal from, 131–32
    unfavorable trends of, 156
    see also conservatism; government;
        libertarianism
Poole, Robert, Jr., 139
pride, 119–120
productivity, 119

Rand, Ayn
    academic philosophers and, 87–90,
        153–55
    affair with Nathaniel Branden of, 5,
        14, 71
    alienation from society of, 14–15,
        147–48
    art defined by, 122
    biographical information on, 11–15,
        127–132
    conservatism attacked by, 133–34
    cruelty in philosophy of, 25–26, 62,
        63, 64, 153
    diet drug used by, 166–67 n5
    epistemology of, 91–98
    ethical innovation of, 98
    feminism in philosophy of, 69–71,
        121
    film experience of, 12, 18, 29, 36–37
    libertarianism attacked by, 137–140
    literary style of, 17–19, 26, 27
    love and sex in philosophy of, 74, 79,
        82–83, 120–21
    loyalty to values as theme of, 28, 31,
        33, 35–36, 42
    metaphysics of, 90–91
    Nietzsche's influence on, 8–9, 16, 21–
        26, 41–43, 167 n1
    Nietzsche rejected by, 47–48, 55, 73,
        120
    personality of, 6–7, 16, 70–71
    political development of, 127–132
    political theory of, 142–47
    repression in fiction of, 48–50, 72–73,
        80–82
    works about, 7–8

rationality, 119
realism (epistemological), 93–95
'Rearden, Henry', 18, 72–73, 81
Red Pawn, 18, 29–30
relativism, 88–90, 154–55
repression, 4–5, 16, 48–50, 72–73, 80–82, 160
reproduction (biological), and ethics, 103, 120–21, 173 n19, 174 n29
rights, 142
'Roark, Howard', 46, 48–50, 66
Romanticism, 123–24
Rothbard, Murray, 4, 138, 139
Russell, Bertrand, 114

sanction of the victim, 59, 84–85, 149–150, 161–62
Schumpeter, Joseph, 176 n5
Schwartz, Peter, 139–140
Schwartz, Wilfred, 15
science, epistemology and, 97–98, 170–71 n9, 171–72 n11, 172 n12
sense of life, 122–25
'Simplest Thing in the World, The', 57–58
skepticism, 88–90, 92, 96–97, 100, 106–08
social contract, 140–41, 142, 144, 177 n12
Social Darwinism, 24, 113
sociobiology, 121

Socrates, 88
Spooner, Lysander, 135

'Taggart, Dagny', 18, 63–65, 68–69, 79–80
Think Twice, 17, 44–45
'Toohey, Ellsworth' 19, 45, 51–52

values (ethical)
    concept of, and life, 100–01, 172–73 n15
    definition of, 100, 172–73 n15
    morality as code of, 99
    see also ethics
Veatch, Henry, 105, 154
volition, 173 n18
We, 57
We the Living, 18, 127
    autobiographical elements in, 33
    characters in, 34–36
    cinematic elements in, 36–37
    editorial changes in, 37–39
    Nietzschean ideas in, 35–40
    plot elements of, 33–34
    publication of, 12
    Red Pawn as sketch for, 30
Weinberg, Alexander, 122
Willkie, Wendell, 128
'Wynand, Gail', 47–48, 49–50

Zamiatin, Yevgeny, 57, 168 n6